Warrior • 118

Byzantine Infantryman

Eastern Roman Empire *c*.900–1204

Timothy Dawson · Illustrated by Angus McBride

First published in Great Britain in 2007 by Osprey Publishing,
Midland House, West Way, Botley, Oxford OX2 0PH, UK
44-02 23rd St, Suite 219, Long Island City, NY 11101, USA
Email: info@ospreypublishing.com

Osprey Publishing is part of the Osprey Group.

Transferred to digital print on demand 2012

First published 2007
3rd impression 2008

Printed and bound by Cadmus Communications, USA

A CIP catalogue record for this book is available from the British Library

ISBN: 978 1 84603 105 2

Page layout by Scribe, Oxford.
Index by Margaret Vaudrey
Originated by PDQ Digital Media Solutions
Typeset in Helvetica Neue and ITC New Baskerville

Artist's note

Readers may care to note that the original paintings from which the colour plates in this book
were prepared are available for private sale. All reproduction copyright whatsoever is retained
by the Publishers. All enquiries should be addressed to:

Scorpio
158 Mill Road
Hailsham
East Sussex
BN27 2SH
UK

Email: scorpiopaintings@btinternet.com

The Publishers regret that they can enter into no correspondence upon this matter.

Acknowledgements

Black and white drawings are by David Irwin.

The Woodland Trust

Osprey Publishing is supporting the Woodland Trust, the UK's leading woodland
conservation charity, by funding the dedication of trees.

www.ospreypublishing.com

COVER IMAGE: **The 10th-century Joshua Casket is a striking
mixture of stylization and realism. The soldiers' quilted
garments are very well rendered. The helms do resemble
other realistic pictures, while their neck hangings are
probably meant to be mail rather than scales. The concave
profile of the shield of the man at the right reflects
descriptions in the manuals. (Metropolitan Museum, NY)**

CONTENTS

BYZANTINE INFANTRYMAN: EASTERN ROMAN EMPIRE c.900–1204

INTRODUCTION

Historical background

The 'fall of the Roman Empire' is by far the most misrepresented event in Western history. The sack of the city of Rome in the early 5th century was certainly a dramatic and tragic event in the life of the empire, but it was by no means 'the end'. Part of the reason for this development was that, since Constantine (Kônstantinos) I had, in AD 330,

The fresco of the Forty Martyrs of Sevastê in the Dovecote Church at Çavusin shows both infantry and cavalry. The foot soldiers' armour is remarkably diverse. The man in the centre is protected by a lamellar *klivanion* supplemented by a skirt of large scales covering his lower belly and groin. (Photograph courtesy of Steven Lowe)

designated the ancient Greek city of Vyzantion (Latin Byzantium) the new capital and renamed it the City of Constantine (Kônstantinopolis), Rome and the western provinces had increasingly diminished in importance in terms of the political and economic life of the empire. It should not be imagined, however, that the elite of Constantinople were content to wave the West goodbye. Imperial forces fought to recover and hold Italy for the empire with varying degrees of success right through to the late 12th century. In fact, the Roman Empire endured for another thousand years until the Ottoman Turks captured Constantinople in 1453. Not even the disaster of the Fourth Crusade was able to break an evolving but continuous heritage of cultural and political transmission. From as early as the 1st century AD the empire's residents called it 'Rômania'. The expression 'Byzantine Empire' did not exist until coined by a German historian in 1557 to embody Western prejudices dating back to the Crusades.

From the late 6th century to the end of the 9th century the concerns of the rulers were rather more pressing and closer to home. After Justinian, the ancient rivalry with Persia dominated military matters, until it was conclusively settled with the destruction of the Sassanian Empire by Emperor Herakleios in 629. Along the way one of the most important monuments of Roman military literature was created around 602, the *Stratêgikon*, sometimes attributed to the emperor and successful general Maurikios. The *Stratêgikon* was to remain influential right through the middle Byzantine period. Reasons for rejoicing were short lived, however, as a new wave of northern barbarians culminated in the Avars besieging the capital itself in 628. The 4th-century walls were more than enough to deter them, despite the fact that they seem to have brought traction trebuchets with them, although the residents of Constantinople themselves were of the opinion that the Virgin Mary, whose likeness had been paraded about the walls, deserved the credit. At about the same time a much more serious threat arose in the East with the advent of Islam. These newly proselytized 'Warriors of God' conquered the southern and eastern provinces in a remarkably short time. It is commonly accepted that resistance in these areas was undermined by widespread disaffection prompted by religious policies emanating from Constantinople, which had tried to impose centralized Orthodoxy on a region that had very diverse traditions of Christianity, as well as substantial enclaves of older religions. The Muslims' successes led to their mounting repeated sieges of the City between 668 and 677. Again, the walls were more than equal to their task, but could not have remained so indefinitely against continuing assaults. The prospect of capture was forestalled by the schism in Islam and ensuing civil war that created the division between Sunni and Shi'a, and ended Muslim expansion into Anatolia. This period of combined external threat and internal division is known today as the Dark Age of Vyzantion, not to be confused with Europe's Dark Ages.

No sooner had stable borders been established with Islam than the empire was wracked internally by an argument over whether the use of religious icons constituted idolatry. The seriousness with which Eastern Orthodoxy of the time took such religious debates, and the fact that the emperor had a crucial role at the centre of the Church, meant that for a century the empire was violently divided against itself. At the end of the 9th century the issue was resolved in favour of icons, and a period of stability and restoration ensued under the Macedonian emperors.

Emperor Leo (Leôn) VI, known (not entirely justly) as 'the Wise', reformed the legal system. More significantly for our interest, he initiated a renewal of the study of military practice at the highest levels. It is evident that while the disruptions of the preceding century had undoubtedly compromised military practice in addition to other areas of life, the development of new techniques and adaptation to new circumstances had continued. Leo's contribution was to have these recorded and codified for the first time since the *Stratêgikon*. Leo's *Taktika* preserves those portions of the *Stratêgikon* that were still relevant, and adds the new developments, including the first mention of lamellar armour. Leo was succeeded by his son, Constantine VII, 'Born in the Purple' (Porphyrogennêtos). Constantine continued his father's literary activities, but on the military side his contribution is confined to a manual on imperial participation in military expeditions, which tells us much about the imperial encampment and arrangements, but nothing about ordinary soldiery.

The third quarter of the 10th century was an erratic period for imperial administration, but important for this study. Two generals who had proved themselves under Constantine VII undertook to write military manuals. The more significant of these was Nikêforos II Fôkas, who had a short period on the imperial throne between 963 and 969. His manual, *A Composition on Warfare* (more commonly known by a modern Latin title, *Praecepta Militaria*) also shows a combination of continuities with and revisions of what had gone before, which tells us much of both his knowledge and his pragmatic experience. The *Taktika* of the second of these later 10th-century generals, Nikêforos Ouranos,

The Roman Empire around the middle of the 11th century, its greatest extent during the middle ages. (Map by John Richards)

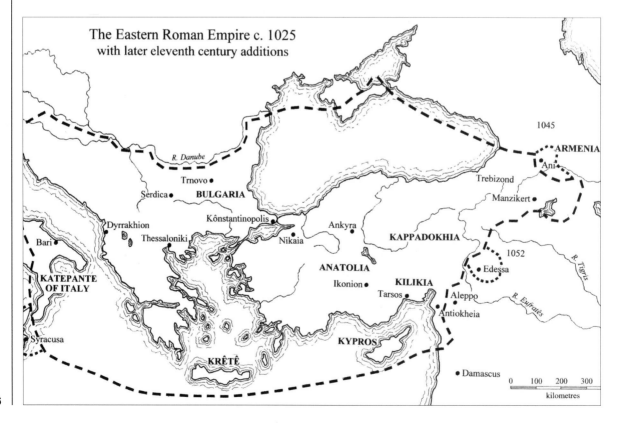

The Eastern Roman Empire c. 1025 with later eleventh century additions

owes a great deal to the *Composition on Warfare*, but also reveals the benefit of Ouranos' campaign experience.

Throughout late antiquity and the earlier middle ages the primary cultural influences on the empire came from the East, especially from Persia, despite the wars and the destruction of the Sassanian Empire, and notwithstanding Iran's incorporation into the new Muslim caliphate. The extent of these influences cannot be underestimated; they took in religion, and diverse aspects of everyday life, especially clothing.

After 976 Basil (Vasileios) II, who had been co-emperor since 963, occupied the imperial throne as the sole or senior emperor. Over the course of 50 years on the 'golden throne' he stabilized imperial administration and campaigned effectively to expand the empire's borders to the greatest extent they had achieved since the 7th century. His most notable success was in defeating the Bulgarians at the battle of Kleidôn in 1014, where he is said to have captured 15,000 of the enemy. The story that he blinded 99 out of 100 and left the remaining man with only one eye to lead them home is doubtful, and his nickname of 'Bulgar-slayer' (Bulgaroktonos) was not invented until the 12th century. Basil was not an innovator by any means. His contribution was to consolidate and consistently implement policies and practices developed or codified in the earlier 10th century.

Empires tend to have a cycle of alternating strong rulers with weak, and the second and third quarters of the 11th century matched the success of Basil's reign with a series of much less effective rulers who ultimately squandered all of Basil's gains and more. Initially events were merely mixed. Large areas of Sicily were gradually wrested from Muslim control, and the Armenian homeland was brought back under imperial sovereignty. In contrast, territory in Italy, recovered for the Roman Empire by Justinian's campaigns of the 6th century, was gradually whittled away by encroachments by the Normans, who went on to take the newly recovered Sicilian possessions, and then turned their greedy eyes towards Greece. There were similar gradual losses in the East, including Antiokheia (modern Antioch) and Armenian Kilikia. The nadir was the disaster of the battle of Manzikert in 1071, which resulted in the loss of the majority of Anatolia to the Seljuk Turks. Shattering as the defeat at Manzikert was, the empire might still have held its core territories but for almost a decade of civil wars as rivals contended for the throne.

These civil wars were eventually won in 1081 by another competent general, Alexios Komnênos, and only just in time, as the Normans set their sights on richer pickings in the Balkans. The civil wars had left the empire impoverished and its army in disarray. Nor were the divisions in the aristocracy really eliminated, yet Alexios was able to fend off the Normans and consolidate his power; again only just in time as the armies of the First Crusade arrived on the borders of the empire. A letter attributed to Alexios allegedly invited these troops to the East, but its authenticity is doubtful; at any rate, either by their very arrival or perhaps because of their unexpectedly large numbers, the early crusaders presented quite a headache. Nevertheless, Alexios proved up to the challenge, moving them on towards Syria, and on the way making good use of them to recover Nikaia for the empire, and extracting a pledge that they would return another recent loss, the city of Antiokheia, to the

A reconstruction of the basic infantryman according to the *Composition on Warfare* of Nikêforos Fôkas. A turban over a thick padded cap, a heavy *kavadion* and a belt-hung *spathion* are as the manuscripts describe, while the boots are the less ideal knee-length *mouzakia* rather than the prefered thigh-length *hypodêmata* illustrated elsewhere. (Author's collection)

control of Constantinople. Until 1118 Alexios continued his work to stabilize the empire both militarily and organizationally.

Contrary to the paradigm referred to earlier, Alexios' two successors both proved to be reasonably effective rulers and competent military commanders. Building upon the stability created by his father, Iôannês II set out to recover lost ground, especially to the East. He regained control of Kilikia, and forced the multi-ethnic Frankish-ruled principality of Antiokheia to honour its pledge of allegiance to Constantinople. Iôannês also seems to have reformed the life of the court, in particular introducing a radical revision of the regalia, which made it less stylized. We can only speculate about how much more he might have achieved had he not died prematurely of a septic accidental arrow wound.

Manuelos Komnênos set out to carry on the good work of his predecessors, but had somewhat mixed results. His early attempt to continue advances in the East by attacking the Seljuk sultanate based in Ikonion (Konya) failed, and there were renewed problems with Western armies travelling East to join the crusades. After this, Manuelos turned his attention to the West and the recovery of territory in Italy. This achieved Roman control of Bari and much of Apulia by 1156, but unfortunately political incompetence by the expeditionary force's commander, which alienated allies, meant that these gains were short lived. Activities in the northern Balkans proved to be rather more successful, culminating in a major victory over the Hungarians at Semlin in 1167. Manuelos is said to have introduced Western practices to the army, although more, it seems, to the cavalry than to the infantry.

The political situation of the empire became increasingly difficult as the 12th century advanced. Assorted Western entities were growing in power. These included the so-called 'Holy Roman Empire', the Norman kingdom incorporating Sicily and portions of southern Italy, and the maritime Italian city states. The growth of the Italian city states, Pisa, Genoa and especially Constantinople's old colony, Venice, was particularly problematical, for they steadily nibbled away the empire's greatest source of wealth – trade – especially in high-value exotic goods such as silk and spices. The emperors tried to use time-honoured military/diplomatic tactics of playing one off against the other. Unfortunately the only way this could be done was by the granting of trade concessions, which only had the result of further reducing Roman revenues from trade and customs duties. Late in his reign Manuelos tried another direction, stripping various Italians of their trading rights and expelling them from the city. This proved in the long term to be even more counterproductive, leading the Italians to redouble their efforts to strip away Roman trade and possessions in the Balkans. The ultimate expression of this was Venice's hijack of the Fourth Crusade to sack Zara and then Constantinople in 1204.

The empire's tendency to look to the East for its models of cultural sophistication had declined in the 11th century. The cultural and intellectual vigour that had characterized the Arab realm in the early centuries of the Islamic era had faded, and al-Islamiyya had much less novelty to offer. The rise of the West and the great movements of crusade and trade meant that some of the need for new ideas began to be satisfied from that direction as the 12th century progressed, although the majority of cultural transmission was still from Rômania to the West.

The last 20 years leading up to the Fourth Crusade were a tragic period. The cycle of bad rulers following good re-asserted itself with a vengeance. The dynasty of the Komnênoi petered out with two emperors who only lasted three years each and achieved nothing good. The rulers of the Angelos family who followed fared little better, as the political elite of the empire were riven with dissension about how to deal with the Western powers and threats. In the Roman Empire such dissension was never merely a matter of debate, but rather one of coups, countercoups and spontaneous civil and military unrest. Thus the elite of the empire proved incapable of forestalling the machinations of the Venetians, and of resisting effectively once the armies of the Fourth Crusade had been diverted against Constantinople, the Queen of Cities.

Military background

The fully professional armies of the Roman republican and early imperial eras were long gone by the beginning of the middle Byzantine era. There were still professional units based in the capital and important cities, but now the majority of any major expeditionary army comprised part-time troops whose families held agricultural land in exchange for military service, further augmented by temporary levies and mercenaries.

It is well known that the backbone of the Roman Army in the earlier period had been the infantry. Cavalry had been the province of foreign auxiliaries to begin with, and even when better established had only very specific and limited roles. The strength of the legion lay in the solidity of the cohort – a mass of armoured men advancing in step behind large shields. No other force of infantry in the known world could match that under normal circumstances. Towards the end of late antiquity the empire faced new threats, and the army confronted unfamiliar military methods. Primary amongst these was the increased use of cavalry amongst Rome's enemies, and not just any cavalry, but heavily armoured horsemen riding armoured horses equipped with stirrups. The Roman Army's

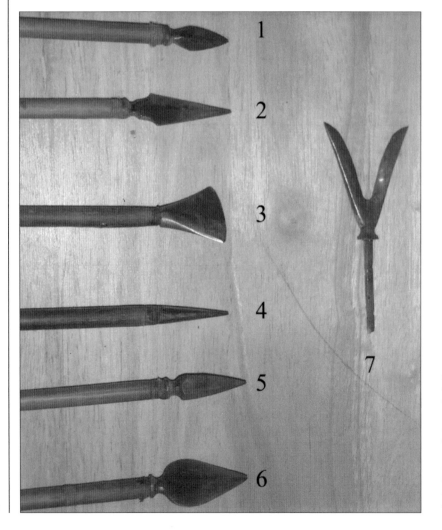

Archaeology has provided ample evidence for arrowheads of this era. A sample are reproduced here. The conical pile (4) and heavy diamond section heads (1 and 5) are those with the most military utility. 2, 3 and 6 were used for hunting terrestrial game and other soft targets, while 7 was used for fowling. (Author's collection)

response to this was to adopt a weapon it had encountered, and indeed defeated, in Greece – the sarissa or pike ('great *kontarion*'). The failure of the sarissa against the manipular legions did not blind the Roman high command to its utility against frontal attacks by heavy cavalry, nor, indeed, against less disciplined and determined foot soldiers. The introduction of the pike in other ways bolstered the army's tried and true methods. Handling a weapon up to 5m (16ft) long demanded a reaffirmation of the rigorous training of old after the laxity lamented by Flavius Vegetius in the 4th century. In particular, the practice of marching in step was essential to making this unwieldy weapon work.

In Graeco-Roman antiquity and the early Roman Empire archery had been the province of barbarian auxiliaries from the north. By the end of late antiquity this had conclusively changed, to such a degree that the author of the *Stratêgikon* could speak of the thumb-draw, devised originally by the nomadic horse-tribes for mounted use, as being the 'Roman draw', in contrast to the three-fingered draw of the Persians.

The Roman adoption of the stirrup in the later 6th century dramatically changed the balance of effectiveness in the forces, making the cavalry the pre-eminent offensive arm in the open battlefield. In the wake of this, the infantry in the field became more of a moving fortress. The infantry formation often served to provide a solid base for the swifter striking of the mounted arm. It also made an essential focus for enemy action, for, of course, Roman cavalry was no less amorphous and capable of an evading countermeasure than that of any other nation. In principle, the infantry retained the same capacity for offensive action it had always had, but the situations in which that offensive capability could be applied were fewer than they had been.

One area in which the pre-eminence of infantry remained unchallenged was in siege warfare, in both offence and defence. The traction trebuchet was introduced from central Asia in the late 6th century and by the beginning of the 7th century was a standard part of the infantry army's expeditionary equipment. Useful as this new weapon was for its relative simplicity and greater throw-weight relative to size, it did not immediately supplant the older torsion artillery by any means. Stone- and arrow-firing *ballistae* (Greek *vallistrai*) might not have the mass impact, but they had an accuracy the traction trebuchet could never match. Its robustness and simplicity almost certainly meant that it replaced the torsion *vallistra* as mobile artillery, relegating it to a defensive role. A technological leap in trebuchet technology came in the 12th century with the invention of the counterweight. The evidence suggests that this was, in fact, a Roman invention. The counterweight remedied the primary failing of the traction trebuchet, namely erratic impulse, and so allowed the weapon to be aimed with some confidence. According to Khoniatês a trebuchet supervised by General Andronikos Kontostephanos was able to accurately strip a wooden gallery from the walls of Zeugminon, thereby sending mocking Hungarian troops to their deaths. The counterweight also allowed larger weapons with greater payloads to be built.

The recovery from the 'Dark Age', the period of external assaults and religious division which began in the 8th century, led the Roman Army to re-acquaint itself with two ancient, oriental forms of armour – scale and lamellar. Both are made of plates of solid material which may be metal, horn or leather and which may be of very similar size, shape and form. The consistent difference between them in our period is that scales were fastened to a single substrate, a garment of cloth or leather, and overlapped downward, while lamellar was first fastened together in rows and then tied together normally overlapping upwards. Like mail, these armours with their numerous, but modestly sized, identical components had the advantage of being amenable to small-scale production units. Unlike mail, they both offered much higher levels of protection. The manuals of the beginning of the 10th century do not make any systematic distinction between infantry and cavalry armour, but the status of the cavalry as the elite arm must have meant that they had first claim on these superior forms of defence, and this is explicitly acknowledged in the later 10th-century manuals. The 11th and 12th centuries were a period of economic growth, and evidence suggests that this meant that some infantry troops were again able to acquire the superior forms of equipment. The Fourth Crusade, the consequential Latin occupation of Constantinople which lasted almost 60 years, and the permanent impoverishment of the empire radically interrupted the culture of the army as much as any area of life; for example, lamellar was never again seen amongst the equipment of the Roman Army.

Force structure and ranks

Any expeditionary force was known as a *tagma* or *Strêlos*. Its size was determined by the nature of the campaign traded off against the economic and logistical constraints on the manpower that could be raised. It was commanded by a *stratêgos* or general. A *tagma* was then divided into a variable number of *meroi* or *tourmai*, each commanded, unsurprisingly, by a *tourmarkhês*. The size of a *meros* or *tourma* varied from 3,000 to 9,000 men, and was divided into three *droungoi*, which similarly would range from 1,000 to 3,000 soldiers. The commander of a *droungos* was a *droungarios*. Below him were several counts (*komêtes*), each commanding a 'banner' (*vandon*) of between 200 and 400 foot soldiers. The traditional unit of a century still existed, called by the Latin-Greek compound *kentarkhion* or the Greek *hekatontarkhion*. Its officer continued to be known by the Hellenized version of the Latin title, *kentêrion* (centurion), and the Latin-Greek hybrid *kentarkhês*, as well as by the Greek *hekatontarkhês*. The century had two divisions, each commanded by a *pentakontarkhês*. Below that were units of eight, *dekarkhia*, and four, *pentarkhia* (the anomaly between the unit names and their numbers is a mystery – if they had ever matched, the units were already smaller by the

A summary of the force structure of an army of this period. The top line names the commanding officer of each unit, while the second line gives the numbers. Only the *meros* was divided into a set number of sub-divisions, that being three. Other units were created in whatever number was required for the manpower available.

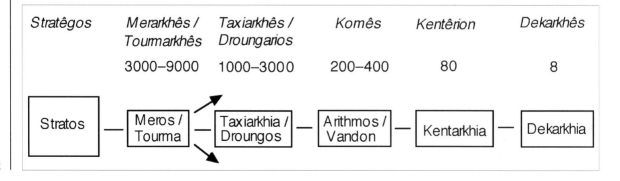

Stratêgos	Merarkhês / Tourmarkhês	Taxiarkhês / Droungarios	Komês	Kentêrion	Dekarkhês
	3000–9000	1000–3000	200–400	80	8
Stratos	Meros / Tourma	Taxiarkhia / Droungos	Arithmos / Vandon	Kentarkhia	Dekarkhia

end of the Roman Republican era), each commanded by a *dekarkhês* or *pentarkhês* respectively, who was counted amongst the number. These officers were denoted by colour-coded sashes. The *dekarkhion* was effectively one of the most important units of the army. Still functioning as the *kontouvernion* (Latin *contubernium*), it remained the primary social unit of the infantry expeditionary army. It was also the main unit of the battle line, functioning as the 'file' (*lokhos*), whose men stood one behind the other to make up the depth of the formation.

The general staff had a full range of functionary ranks. *Mandatôres* carried the orders down the chain of command. *Minsôres* or *minsouratôres* were surveyors who went ahead of the marching army to lay out the camp. There were also banner-bearers (*vandoforoi*) and trumpeters (*voukinatôr*). Training was supervised by drill-masters called *kampidoktores*, who carried a distinctive baton named a *kampidiktorion*.

CHRONOLOGY

*c.*602	The completion of the *Stratêgikon* often attributed to Maurikios establishes the pre-eminence of the cavalry as the premier offensive segment of the Roman Army.
628	Avars besiege Constantinople.
633–50	Loss of Roman possessions in Syria and Egypt.
668–77	Repeated Muslim sieges of Constantinople.
886–912	Leo VI ('the Wise'/Sophos).
*c.*895	Composition of the *Taktika* of Leo.
913–99	Constantine VII ('Born in the Purple'/Porphyrogennêtos). Constantine VII presided over a veritable imperial publishing industry, including a detailed treatise on imperial military expeditions and an inventory of the materiel of the Cyprus Expedition.
939	A large expedition is launched with the aim of taking Cyprus back from the Muslims. It was unsuccessful.
*c.*950	Likely date for the composition of the *Syllogê Taktikôn*.
959–63	Rômanos II.
963–69	Nikêforos Fôkas co-emperor with Basil II. *The Composition on Warfare* (*Praecepta Militaria*) appears to have been written while Nikêforos was emperor.
963–1015	Basil II (later called 'the Bulgar-slayer'/Bulgaroktonos) co-emperor with Nikêforos Fôkas and later with Iôannês I Tzimiskês.
969–76	Iôannês I Tzimiskês becomes co-emperor with Basil II.
999–1007	Nikêforos Ouranos serves as governor of the province of Antiokheia in Syria. His *Taktika* was composed during this period.
1014	Basil II crushes the forces of the Bulgarian kingdom at the battle of Kleidôn. Bulgaria never again poses any serious threat to the empire.
1020s	First Norman incursions into Roman territory in southern Italy.
1025–28	Constantine VIII ('Born in the Purple'/Porphyrogennêtos).
1028–34	Rômanos III Argyros.
1034–41	Mikhailos IV ('the Paphlagonian'/Paphlagonos).
1038–43	Eastern Sicily recovered from Muslim control. Shortly afterwards lost again to Norman encroachment.
1042	Zôê ('Born in the Purple'/Porphyrogennêta).
1042–54	Constantine IX ('the Duellist'/Monomakhos). How this emperor got his nickname is a mystery, for he had no particular martial talent.
1045	Armenian heartland re-incorporated into the empire.
1052	Edessa and surrounding region re-incorporated into the empire.
1055–56	Theodôra ('Born in the Purple'/Porphyrogennêta).
1056–57	Mikhailos VI Bringas.
1057–59	Isaakios I Komnênos.
1059–67	Constantine X Doukas.

1067–71	Rômanos IV Diogenês.
1070s	Norman expansion begins to encroach on Roman territory in the Balkans.
1071	Roman Army severely defeated by the Seljuk Turks at Manzikert due to divisions in command. Rômanos IV Diogenês captured and shortly afterwards killed. This defeat resulted in the permanent loss of most of the empire's Anatolian territory.
1071	Normans capture Bari, the last Roman outpost in Italy.
1071–78	Mikhailos VII Doukas. Mikhailos VII attempted to curb Norman incursions by diplomatic methods, particularly by a marriage alliance.
1078–81	Nikêforos III Botaneiatês. During Botaneiatês' reign the Normans resume their encroachments onto the Greek islands.
1081	An army led by Alexios I is defeated by Normans at Dyrrakhion. Infantry in the campaign seems to have been dominated by the Varangians who suffered major losses.
1081–1118	Alexios I Komnênos. Alexios won out after a period of civil war that severely damaged the army, and led to a dramatic increase in the use of foreign mercenaries in preference to regular Roman troops.
1098	The armies of the First Crusade arrive at Constantinople. Alexios hastens them across the Bosforos into Anatolia and sends them to recapture Nikaia from the Turks. Roman forces pre-empt the storming of the city by the crusaders by taking the Nikaian surrender directly. This caused considerable resentment amongst the Westerners, and a pretext for their repudiating agreements they had made, notably to return Antiokheia to the control of Constantinople.
1118–43	Iôannês II Komnênos.
1138	Iôannês II leads a large army to the east, re-asserting Vyzantion's suzerainty over Armenian Kilikia and the crusader principality of Antiokheia. During this expedition nobles of the Constantinopolitan court competed against those of Antiokheia in the first recorded tournament in the East.
1143	Iôannês dies of septicaemia resulting from a wound from his own arrows whilst out hunting during a campaign.
1143–80	Manuelos I Komnênos. Manuelos continued his father's generally effective campaigning to both East and West, and is credited with Westernizing the military methods used by the army. Manuelos entered into an alliance with the German 'Holy Roman' Empire against the Hohenstaufen kingdoms of Sicily and Italy.
1147	Launching of the Second Crusade.
1148	Normans commence permanent occupation of territory on the Greek mainland.
1153–56	Imperial troops attempt to regain control of southern Italy. Initially successful, the campaign ended with defeat at Brindisi.
1156	Kilikian Armenians under T'oros rebel against imperial rule.
1158	Manuelos brings rebellious Kilikia back under the control of Constantinople.
1159	In the wake of the end of the Kilikian rebellion Reynald de Chatillon, Prince of Antiokheia, makes submission to the emperor, who enters the city in triumph.
1176	Turks inflict a severe defeat on the Roman Army at Myriokefalon. This ends attempts to recover the Anatolian losses of the battle of Manzikert.
1180–83	Alexios II Komnênos.
1182	Western residents of Constantinople are massacred in a riot which may have had imperial backing.
1182–85	Andronikos I Komnênos. Andronikos tried to reform the bureaucracy and reduce the influence of the great families and of Westerners. His repressive measures alienated the aristocracy and then the populace, leading to his overthrow.
1184	Andronikos makes an alliance with Sala'ad-din which would have partitioned the Levant between the empire and the Ayyubid sultanate.
1185–95	Isaakios II Angelos. Isaakios and his son Alexios III had no ability in or inclination towards administration and presided over a regime of excess and dissolution which further weakened the empire.

1195–1203 Alexios III Angelos. Friction and violence between the natives and Western residents within the empire increase.

1203–04 Isaakios II again (co-emperor: Alexios IV). Isaakios II was reinstated by Western intervention, but the demands of the foreigners offended the populace, who rejected these rulers and elevated the anti-Western Alexios Mourtzouphlos.

1204 Alexios V Mourtzouphlos. The empire was now too weak to make any serious resistance to Western forces and fell to the hijacked Fourth Crusade in April 1204.

RECRUITMENT

The sources of manpower drawn upon by the army through this period were very diverse from the beginning, and were as subject to change across the time as other aspects of the army and society. The manuals are clear on certain points, however. For example, only the best physical specimens were preferred, and they should be no older than 40 years of age. Recruits ought also, as far as could be determined, to be of good character.

At the beginning of the 10th century the thematic forces that made up the bulk of the army were drawn from a pool of 'stratiotic' families who held *strateia*, that is, who owed military service in connection with tenure of land. The sources primarily discuss this in relation to cavalry where they mention categories of soldiery at all, but it is likely that it would also have applied to the front-line infantry as well. *Strateia* was hereditary, passing from one individual to another within a family. These men were recorded on the *adnoumia* or muster rolls maintained by the provincial commander. In maintaining this pool of manpower it was deemed important to consider both the physical fitness and capacity of the individual and his moral and social probity. Serious crimes were cause for the registered man to be struck off the roll. In such a case, his obligation would be transferred in the first instance to another suitable member of his (extended) family, or, if no such person were available, it would be temporarily or permanently assigned elsewhere. Similarly, the *strateia* would be reassigned where such a family died out. Where possible, an empty *strateia* would be transferred to a stratiotic household who had gained members who could discharge the service. Otherwise, it would be assigned to another capable local family, either voluntarily or by imposition. Another option exercised from the capital was to resettle areas where there was a quantity of stratiotic lands in need of tenancy. Such settlers could be drawn from other areas within the empire, a policy that was sometimes used to alleviate overpopulation, and at others times to forestall potential dissension. Resettlement was repeatedly imposed upon segments of the Armenian population for this reason. Other settlers were immigrants to the empire, such as the Arab tribe called Banu Habib which was taken in by Constantine VII. Remarkably, one last category of settler given stratiotic lands comprised prisoners of war.

The sources of recruits for the standing tagmatic units were equally various. Just as in many other societies right up to today, military service must have been an attractive option for males who found themselves short of prospects. In the countryside, this was not so much a matter of the 'younger son syndrome' seen in the West, since inheritance of land within the empire was partitive rather than singly by primogeniture, so it must have been more a matter of choice on the one hand, or dire necessity in some cases where partitive inheritance would render a farm too small to be viable. Tagmatic forces were also composed to some degree of foreign troops. It is not entirely suitable to characterize these as 'mercenaries', since at this time such foreigners were incorporated into the Roman Army's established structure and methods, rather than forming their own units. A better modern comparison might be the Ghurkas in the British Army, as the foreigners serving in the imperial army likewise often came from places with a long-standing and quasi-colonial relationship with Constantinople. Examples of this include, again, the Armenians, and also the Georgians, Bulgarians and peoples of southern Rus.

The final class of troops not included in these groups was the light infantry (*psiloi*) – archers, javelineers and slingers – whose service did not require the level of skill and drill of the regular soldiery. While a small number of these troops would have been maintained in tagmatic divisions, generally they must have been recruited or conscripted at need and for the duration of a campaign from any pool of marginal manpower. In civilian life these men pursued lowly skilled occupations such as those of street porters, construction labourers, woodcutters and so on.

Soldiery was not all the army needed, of course. There was also the support staff, such as muleteers and waggoners, and each *kontouvernion* had a servant. As with the lights, the *tagmata* must have routinely had some of these drawn from the same sources as the troops themselves. For thematic expeditions such ancillary manpower would have been levied from amongst the local population. Often these functions must have been filled by youths or boys from stratiotic households who were too young yet to take up full military duties. It is also possible that some stratiotic families may have specialized in transport provision, just as many specialized in cavalry.

APPEARANCE

In contrast to the intricate rules that governed clothing for civilian men, especially in the court context, the military manuals have little specific to say about the dress of the troops. But their scanty information can be supplemented from other sources. The *Stratêgikon* had recommended 'Gothic' tunics for the infantry in place of the 'Avar' tunics of the cavalry, the distinction probably being that the cavalry tunics were split in the centre, a feature already shown in late antique art, while the infantry tunics had a continuous skirt. This distinction certainly survived in civilian dress in our period, and doubtless did in military practice as well. The manuals are unanimous in recommending that military garments should not reach below the knee, in the manner of labouring men and in contrast to the dominant civilian fashion for men of status to wear ankle-length tunics. The manuals stress that in appearance the troops should be neat and well presented, observing that, just as in more recent armies, these qualities are bound up inextricably with morale, and hence combat effectiveness. Beyond these considerations, the sources do not strongly suggest a high degree of uniformity in the dress

of the soldiery. It is likely that it depended upon how much centralized or centrally coordinated supply could be mobilized by the officer organizing a unit. Most probably there was a conspicuous division between metropolitan tagmatic and provincial thematic units, with the former tending to uniformity following the example set at court, and the latter to diversity.

The popularly accepted image of tunics in the Eastern Roman Empire is rather stuck in a late antique time warp. By the 10th century much had changed. Rather than the shapeless 'Coptic' sacks of old Rome, men of Constantinople wore tunics and shirts tailored and fitted in a sophisticated manner. They were cut high on the neck, opening down from the left side in a style that went back to ancient Persia, and *esoforia* (shirts) were finished with a low collar. The sleeves extended fully over the wrist and the cuffs were close fitting and sometimes had a short opening fastened even more tightly to the wrist with a single button. At court all the men of a particular rank or function wore tunics of the same colour, and, while this is not mentioned in the sources, it is likely that in the centralized supply of tagmatic units this paradigm was followed, especially in view of their occasional appearance in imperial ceremonies.

Vegetius had recommended that the type of hat called 'Pannonian' should be worn by the soldiers when they were not wearing helmets. The hat of cylindrical appearance which is commonly associated with this term was still in use in the 10th to 12th centuries, and more detailed representations of this era show that it was not a true *pyxis* (pill-box) shape but rather a deep round-ended cylinder with the closed end on the head and the open end turned up outside to conceal the crown. A variety of other hats were popular through the period, although no others had specifically military associations. Doubtless the thick felt caps which served as helmet linings and turban bases were worn much of the

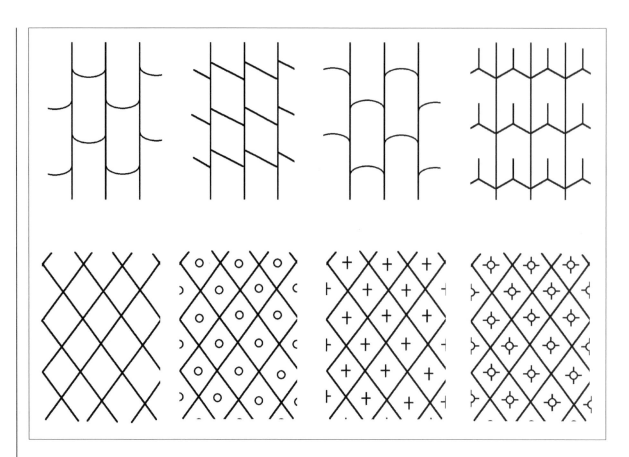

time by troops, as, indeed, must also have been the turbans wrapped directly on the head that were common to civilian fashion.

A number of other fashions known from civilian contexts had military utility as well. The old Roman disdain for the barbarians' trousers had taken on a new lease of life with the adoption of the Persian habit of wearing leggings over lighter breeches. By the 10th century, even in civilian use, the leggings could be padded with wool, cotton or even silk floss. This was simply as protection from the cold for civilians, but would be even more valuable as a supplement to leg protection for soldiers. The likelihood of such leggings, which were originally called *kampotouva*, or 'field-hose', being in common military use is confirmed by the fact that even the emperor would wear them as part of his military regalia from time to time.

Not surprisingly, the manuals give more attention to the troops' footwear than to any other aspect of clothing, for nothing, short of starvation, is more damaging to an army on campaign than poor footwear. Nikêforos Fôkas recommends thigh boots as the ideal for the infantry, with the upper part to be folded down onto the shin for ease of marching, and back up over the knee to provide protection in battle. This may have relied simply upon the weight and stiffness of the leather, like later European thigh boots, or they may already have been tied up to the trouser cord, as begins to be illustrated in the 13th century. Calf-length boots (*mouzakia*) were the next best thing, with low shoes (*sandalia*) a poor third. The *Syllogê Taktikôn* recommends that the troops' footwear should be fitted with a modest number of hobnails, saying that this is best for marching – quite unlike the excesses of early imperial Roman habits in this area! The archaeology of the late antique cemeteries of Egypt shows that Near Eastern footwear technology was far ahead of Europe. Patterns much like many still in use today were employed, and more substantial shoes and boots had thick, multi-layered soles better suited to walking over the drier and more rocky landscapes of the Levant.

Although, as noted above, padded garments were in civilian use even at the beginning of this period, the thick padded garment (*zava* or *kavadion*) which was the most basic protection of the *hoplitês* and *peltastos*, and which doubtless predominated in some units, was probably a specialized item more commonly supplied by central arrangement and so likely to be more uniform in their appearance, perhaps like the tunics of a common colour. The fact that the manuals are very detailed about the form of these coats supports the likelihood of their being a uniform supply item. Ample pictorial sources give the common quilting patterns used on these garments. They were normally vertical linear compartments cross-quilted in various ways to forestall slippage of the cotton wadding, but there are hints that the parade version of the padded garments (*gounia*) might be quilted in more decorative arabesque patterns.

Officers were set apart by wearing a cloth sash tied around the torso, called *pektorarion*. These sashes must have been colour coded for different ranks, but unfortunately there is no record of the precise correlations, which were probably either dictated by custom or else set ad hoc in a given expeditionary army.

One aspect of uniformity is explicitly recommended in the manuals, and that is that all the shields of each unit be painted the same. In addition, although not mentioned in the literature, pictorial sources quite often show similarities between the way the shields are painted and the patterning on the main field of the common form of banner. So it is possible that they were also coordinated, thus helping to cement the cohesion of the company in battle.

One very conspicuous aspect of the troops' appearance stems from the admonition that idle time in camp was to be occupied in keeping arms and armour polished. Besides forestalling the 'devil's work', well-maintained kit, like the clothing mentioned above, was both an expression of, and a factor in, good morale.

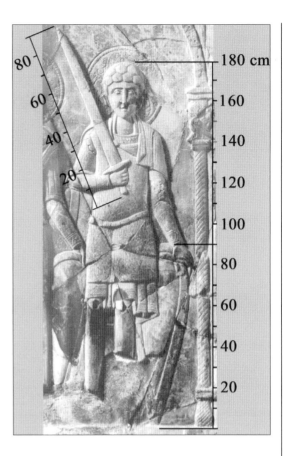

The scale superimposed on this soapstone carving of a military saint illustrates how realistic some pictures of this era can be. The proportions of the equipment precisely match the sizes specified in military manuals. His scale shirt is clearly that of an infantry soldier, as is the tear-drop shield. (Background picture: Hermitage Museum, St Petersburg)

EQUIPMENT

The military manuals surviving from the 10th century offer quite a variable picture of the equipment their authors thought the troops should have. Evidence from other sources of the 10th to 12th centuries is similarly mixed, yet the very diversity of the evidence undoubtedly

reflects the practical reality of the situation. Hence, the range of equipment described here should be taken as a repertoire from which supply officers and the men themselves picked and chose as their resources and preferences allowed.

In terms of the ideals decreed by the manuals, it is noteworthy that Leo's *Taktika* and the *Syllogê Taktikôn* foresee the potential for a much higher quality of protective equipment than do Nikêforos Fôkas and Nikêforos Ouranos later in the century. The former propose armour approximating to that of the cavalry with cloth armours as a fall-back position, whereas the latter only mention padding for the infantry.

Headgear

Known archaeological survivals of helms from this period are depressingly rare, and the artistic conventions of the time also mean that they are infrequently illustrated. Such evidence as there is, however, does paint a picture largely of developmental continuity with late antiquity. Most prevalent is a simplified form of the five-piece ridge helm known from several 4th-century examples found at Intercisa. The barbarian *spangenhelm* also continues in use, now, like the ridge helms, bereft of cheek plates. The taller more pointed form of *spangenhelm* commonly known as 'Caucasian' due to the numerous 10th- to 11th-century examples found in Russia and the Ukraine was also probably in use from the beginning of the period, although it is not illustrated in East Roman art until the 11th century. The unique survival known as the 'Yasenovo helm' attributed to the 9th or 10th century is quite a different construction to those types. Whether it is genuinely an innovation is uncertain, however. The reinforcing bands across the crown hark back to the modifications made to legionary helmets in the early 3rd century to counter the power of the Dacian falx, but may just be a pragmatic response to a similar threat. Pictures in the illustrated manuscript of the chronicle of Skylitzes show that forms like the Yasenovo helm must have been almost as widespread as the ridge helm. In the scaled-down plans of the later 10th century, infantry troops were

Despite all the anti-Constantinople rhetoric that appears in Frankish sources, the residents of the crusader states recognized the vastly superior cultural sophistication of the Eastern Roman Empire and constantly looked to it for example in both civilian matters and military. The psalter made for Queen Melisende of Jerusalem in the 12th century embodies this strikingly. This detail of the carved ivory front cover shows a man clad in the basic equipment of a Roman infantryman extending back as far as the 7th century – a conical *spangenhelm* and a hooded *zava* (arming tunic) quilted in a typically Byzantine manner. (© British Library)

A characteristic construction of scale armour from surviving Roman examples. The padding cord served two purposes – one was to protect the laces binding the metal to the garment, the other was to obstruct any point that might slip up under the scales.

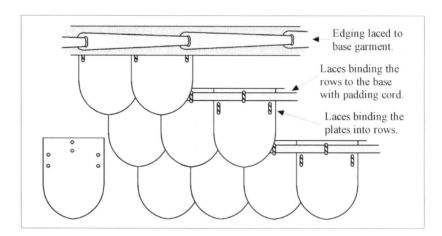

Edging laced to base garment.

Laces binding the rows to the base with padding cord.

Laces binding the plates into rows.

expected to have nothing more substantial than a very thick felt cap with a copious turban wound over the top.

In the 12th century we seem to see some innovations coming in, although whether they arise within the empire, or are imported very rapidly from neighbours, or merely begin to be illustrated belatedly is not clear. One is the appearance of early forms of 'kettle-hat' – one-piece helms with a slight brim. The manifest long-term collective memory of the Roman Army may mean that this was a revival based upon remembered forms, or even that brimmed forms had never fallen completely out of use. The other innovation might also be a revival of a remembered ancient form. The Phrygian cap-style helm sweeps the Mediterranean in the 12th century with no regard for cultural boundaries.

All these might be worn plain, or over a separate hood of mail, known in the Roman Empire since late antiquity, but they would often carry some form of attached neck protection. The ridge helms seem commonly to have borne a padded skirt. The quilting patterns shown on these are often suggestive of *pteruges* (hanging leather strips), and it is possible that such *pteruges* may sometimes have been used as a low-grade substitute for the more protective padding. Phrygian cap helms also show these forms of neck protection at times. The surviving Caucasian helms seem routinely to have carried a mail skirt, either linked on through holes punched in the rim, as with some of the early medieval European *spangenhelm*s, or attached by a more sophisticated method whereby the edge was rolled into a tube, then cut into a comb with the mail strung on a wire threaded through the comb. This suspension

This centurion at the Crucifixion depicted in the 'Hidden Church' (Tokali Kiliesi) at Göreme wears a *klivanion* of lamellar with separate splinted sleeves. The patterning on his undergarment represents one of the more intricate quilting patterns, since brocade cloths in such diapered patterns were not yet being produced at this time. (Photograph courtesy of Steven Lowe)

system is also found on the Yasenovo helm. Illustrations of the early brimmed helms also show mail hangings, but without any indication as to how they were attached.

Body armour

The trend for substituting soft armours for metal and leather seems to have started in late antiquity. The early forms were heavy wool felt faced with woven cloth, and this construction is still mentioned by Leo at the beginning of our period. The cultivation of cotton appears to have exploded across the Levant in the 10th century and as a result raw cotton wadding rapidly supplanted wool felt as the padding of choice. Arming garments came in two main forms reflecting the division in men's civilian clothing – pull-over tunic (*zava*) and button-up coat (*kavadion*). The greater vulnerability of having an opening in the front could be obviated by using one of the long-established Persian ways of making a coat double-breasted with the outer edge falling from the left side of the neck. Fastening was by buttons that could be metal, wood or bone, or a 'Chinese knot', which passed through a loop rather than a buttonhole. Sleeves on these garments could be just elbow length, although this seems to have been primarily intended for padding under more solid armours. More usually, padded coats to be worn alone by infantry had full-length sleeves with which mobility was optimized by an opening to pass the arms, either in the elbow according to the *Syllogê Taktikôn* and Leo, or in the armpit according to the Nikêforoi. The loose part of the sleeves was then to be buttoned up behind the shoulder to get it out of the way. The utility of this arrangement must have been that, in addition to battlefield protection, these arming coats were to afford harsh weather protection as well. (An expedient one still sees adopted by re-enactors today!) To this end it is very likely that the lower portion of the sleeves was long enough to cover the hands as well, in a practice that is likewise seen in civilian dress. Emperor Nikêforos states that the coats were to be covered with raw silk and be 'as thick as may be stitched', that is perhaps as much as 5cm (nearly 2in.).

Mail (*lôrikion alusidôton*, literally 'chain armour') was just as ubiquitous in the Eastern Roman Empire as it was in the medieval West. The generic type of a pull-on shirt ending somewhere on the thigh with elbow-length sleeves was the norm for infantry across the period here as well.

Scale armour (*lôrikion folidôton*) is another style which probably never fell out of use from the early imperial era. No middle Byzantine period pieces are known to have been found, so the precise form and construction are unknown, but pictorial sources suggest no notable differences from examples from adjacent cultures. The overall form of scale defences appears the same as for mail – a pull-on shirt ending somewhere on the thigh with elbow-length sleeves. In the case of a shortage of metal, scale armours could be made of horn or ox hide.

Lamellar (*klivanion*) was another armour known to the early imperial Roman Army, but it seems to have fallen out of use amidst the tribulations of the fall of the West. By the beginning of the 10th century it had returned, and rapidly underwent a series of technological refinements which produced distinctively Byzantine types. The widespread form by which it was known to the early Romans was entirely laced. The 10th-century innovations start to make it into something like an inside-out brigandine, initially laced then riveted to a leather backing before suspending the rows. The complexity and hence expense of making a *klivanion* probably mean it was never commonly in use for infantry, despite the earlier sources.

Limb armour

Leo and the *Syllogê Taktikôn* in their ambitious way refer to the troops having defences for the forearms (*manikellia*) and for the lower legs (*podopsella*). A few pictures, particularly from the latter part of our period, do show rather awkward looking lower leg armour as slightly tapered, square-ended solid tubes. In addition to these, splinted defences were certainly in use. The Aght'amar Goliath wears *manikellia* laminated down the arm, rather than along it like splints, a method which looks forward to forms we might tend to think of as Ottoman.

The scaled-down expectations of the Nikêforoi later in the 10th century leave foot soldiers with no recommended protection for the lower arms. This was not an entirely unreasonable approach when the primary weapon was a long pike, and hand weapon combat a last resort. Protection for the legs was to be afforded ideally by long, heavy boots, which had a section that could be brought up over the knee onto the thigh in combat, and folded down onto the shin for ease of movement when marching.

Curiously absent from the military manuals, but discussed in some detail in other literary sources are *kampotouva*, or 'field-hose', that is to say, padded leggings. These were in civilian use, and formed an essential part of the emperor's military-related regalia, so it is hard to imagine that their military utility had been forgotten.

Shields

As usual, the range of shields shown in art is narrower that that referred to in literature. The term *skoutarion* is applied to both round shields and the tear-drop shape that had evolved from the oval scuta of antiquity. Pictorial sources show both forms as being fully convex. Round *skoutaria* could be domed or conical in section. They could be up to 90cm (35in.) in diameter according to the manuals, although those shown in art tend to be smaller, a more practical 75–80cm (30–31½in.). The section of the tear-drop *skoutarion* was strongly curved at the broad top, tapering smoothly to the point at the bottom. Long *skoutaria* could be as much as 110cm (43in.) long, but, again, a more practical 95cm (37in.) is common to the majority of manuals and art. All forms of *skoutarion* were fitted with a pair of rope or leather handles attached separately at each

Corroborating the Goliath of Aght'amar, this St George wears a *klivanion* of lamellar running continuously down onto his thighs rather than ending at the hips, and so unmistakably made for an infantryman. Note also the sleeves of his padded undergarment emerging from the sleeves of the *klivanion*. An 11th-century fresco in the Church of Hasan Dagi, Kappadokhia. (Photograph courtesy of Steven Lowe)

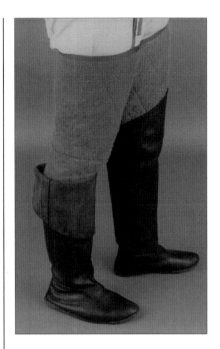

Nikêforos Fôkas recommended that the infantry ought to wear long boots which would protect the knee and lower thigh in battle, but which could be folded down for ease of movement on the march. This reconstruction uses a pattern based upon a 12th-century soapstone carving of a military saint. (Author's Collection)

end to rings fixed into the body of the shield, and gripped in one fist without any forearm contact. It seems clear that these shields were commonly built on a base of cane or wickerwork like the practice shields mentioned by Vegetius. There was also a large rectangular shield called a *thureos* which was probably used as a more static defence in the manner of the later Western pavise.

Weaponry

Archery equipment comprised a composite recurve bow and case, arrows and quiver, and a *sôlênarion* with its darts in their own pouch. The Roman bow was about 1m (just over 3ft) long when strung, and smoothly recurved, rather than having distinct 'ears' in the Central Asian style. The foot archer's bowcase was slung from a shoulder strap, in contrast to the belt-hung horse archer's type, but also carried the strung bow. Arrows for military use carried a variety of heads from the general-purpose smooth conical pile to heavy, multifaceted armour-piercing bodkins. Archers carried lighter, bladed and barbed heads for hunting as well. Flights were a symmetrical crescent shape and quite small. In keeping with the necessities of the thumb-draw, arrows were fletched with four feathers. Like the bowcase, the infantry quiver was hung from a shoulder strap, and the rare illustrations show it as being a round-bottomed cylinder with arrows inserted point downwards, the opposite way to cavalry practice. It is impossible to know the exact form of the *sôlênarion* darts, but it seems likely that they were about 15cm (6in.) long, fitted with two flights parallel to the nock, and conical piles.

The *Syllogê Taktikôn* advises that javelins be no longer than 2.35m (7ft 9in.) overall, which seems surprisingly long, and implies that these must be quite light in their shafts and heads. Pictorial sources indicate that javelin heads were of the same socketed form as other spears, with no hint of the survival of the old Roman *pilum*.

Again according to the *Syllogê Taktikôn*, slings should be 1.2m (4ft) long. This suggests that the weapon in question was a staff sling rather

This fragment of a 6th-century mosaic from the Great Palace corroborates the assertion in the *Stratêgikon* that the thumb-draw was established as the preferred Roman method very early. It also shows some good detail of the type of bow in use. (Author's Collection)

than the ancient thong sling. Staff slings allow for a heavier projectile and require much less space in which to operate, which must have been a consideration in the formations known to have been in use.

Spears came in three types. The small or peltast spear (*kontarion mikron*) was 2.5m (just over 8ft) long. The large or hoplite spear or pike was between 4m and 5m (approximately 13ft and 16ft 6in.) long. The only stipulation for the heads of these spears was that they ought to be 'fit for the task'. The *menavlion* was also a short spear, but very heavy. The manuals recommend that it should be made from a whole sapling rather than cut timber, and that the head should be 25–40cm (10–15½in.) long.

Bladed hand weapons came in considerable variety. Light troops carried a long, heavy single-edged knife like a machete, which probably tended to serve as a tool more than a weapon. Swords existed in two primary forms, the straight, double-edged *spathion* and the slightly curved single-edged *paramêrion*. Both were used by infantry. These swords could be hung either from a shoulder strap (baldric) or from a waist belt. In the case of the *spathion*, the choice of suspension method determined how the sword hung. The attachment points for a baldric were opposite each other on either side of the scabbard as with the old *gladius*, and so the weapon hung vertically by the leg. The attachments for the belt-hung (*zôstikion*) *spathion* were on the same side of the scabbard, and therefore the sword hung close to horizontal. Hanging points for the *paramêrion* were the same for either suspension method, on the same side of the scabbard, and hence the sword hung close to horizontal 'beside the thigh', a literal translation of the name.

Axes were another staple of the foot soldier. These, too, came in quite a variety, ranging from modest single-bladed hatchets to substantial double-bladed battle axes. The main blade on the battle axe type varied from somewhat flared to a full almost semicircular crescent like the later Eastern *tabar*. The secondary fitting could be the same, or else a hammerhead, a spike or a blade like a spear point. Combat axes

The *sôlênarion* at full draw
ready to loose the projectile.
(Author's Collection)

The *sôlênarion* at full draw ready to loose the projectile. (Author's Collection)

were always single handed to allow the use of a shield. Double-handed axes were carried in the army's kit, but only used for timber cutting. Maces were not a normal part of the foot soldier's armoury.

Artillery

An expeditionary force normally set out with some artillery – the *vallistra* and trebuchet (Greek *alakation*) are specified by the manuals. The torsion-powered arrow-shooting *vallistra* was still widely used at least to the middle of the 11th century, and probably continued to 1204, albeit becoming more and more rare. The older forms of stone-throwing devices had been superseded in the 6th century by the traction trebuchet which offered much simpler construction and operation combined with greater throw-weights. This became outmoded itself in the early 12th century by the counterweight trebuchet which gave repeatable accuracy to the cast, and the possibility of building even larger and more powerful devices. Present evidence suggests that the counterweight trebuchet was a Roman invention.

The precise methods by which Greek Fire and other incendiary weapons were deployed is still something of a vexed question. Siegecraft manuals of the 10th century do show pictures of individual soldiers using portable flame-throwers, which look remarkably like old-fashioned fire extinguishers – a cylinder with a nozzle at one end and a plunger handle at the rear – but whether this is a flight of the artist's imagination is unknown. It might well have been possible for a flammable liquid to be loaded into such a portable syringe device for human deployment via siege towers. Ignition could then have been by another man carrying a torch, or, if one form of Greek Fire was a phosphoros-based system as has been theorized, then the mixture would ignite spontaneously on contact with air.

TRAINING

The Roman Army of the 10th century embodied an uninterrupted heritage of methods dating back into antiquity. The formation manoeuvres described in the *Stratêgikon* attributed to Emperor Maurikios (which was still being copied extensively in the 10th and 11th centuries) which are referred to in passing in the new manuals of the 10th century manifestly assume, for example, that the troops are still well drilled to march in step. Any attempt to counter march with *kontaria* around 4.5m (nearly 15ft) long is doomed to failure without such a level of training. Hence, much essential practice was evidently transmitted orally, and so for an insight into the basic training of the individual soldier we must turn to Vegetius, whose methods are unlikely to have been substantially altered. According to *Epitoma Rei Militaris*, a new recruit underwent two sessions of training a day, which involved first marching and leaping to develop his fitness, agility and coordination, and then drills with weapons and shield. Experienced troops trained once a day, requiring more to maintain their skills than to develop them. Vegetius suggests that drills were to be done with practice weapons and shields that were twice the weight of the real thing. Although 10th-century sources do mention wooden practice weapons, this aspect of training was probably not continued in the middle Byzantine era, partly because of constraints of finance and supply, and partly because such weapons as the pike or *menavlion* would have been impossible for any man to handle if made double their normal weight. Adding to these exercises, Leo advises that the troops should be made to run across broken ground, and up and down hills. From the earliest stage of training the soldiery was accustomed to recognizing commands transmitted by trumpet, horn or drum. These essential elements of basic training must have been common to all classes of infantry, whether *hoplitês*, *peltastês* or *psilos*.

With its (for the West) unusual globular pommel and inlays reminiscent of marginal figures in Byzantine manuscripts, this 11th-century sword in the Army Museum, Paris is likely to have originated in the Eastern Roman Empire. (Author's Collection)

According to Vegetius, side-arms training consisted of attacking a post, practising to move in quickly, make an effective attack and move out with equal speed whilst preserving shield defence, and it is likely that this custom continued alongside man-to-man training. Vegetius refers to set exercises called *armatura*, which must have been something like shadow-boxing or the *kata* of oriental martial arts, and this type of training may also have continued. Training was supervised by drill-masters known as *kampidoktores* (literally 'learned in the field'), who carried a swagger-stick (*kampidiktorion*) which they doubtless used to 'encourage' trainees to greater efforts!

Art works of this era indicate the existence of sophisticated sword and shield techniques. Two forms are in evidence, one in which the shield was kept close to maximize protection against other weapons, such as spears and projectiles, and another style in which the shield was held in an extended position to facilitate maximum offensive capability. The latter style distinctly presages techniques shown in later European manuals. Leo recommends that to hone their side-arm skills and fitness, heavy troops were to engage in single combats in full armour with their shields and wooden practice weapons in place of their lethal armament. Another ancient technique requiring systematic training which continued in use was the 'turtle' (Latin *testudo*), now called *foulkon*, whereby a tight formation held shields above as well as to the front and sides in order to advance under heavy missile attack.

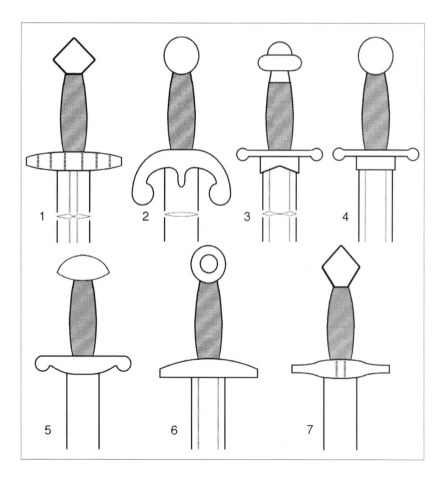

Examples of sword fittings shown in pictorial sources. 1 and 2: 10th century (ivory triptychs, Hermitage and Louvre). The resemblance between 2 and the jinete swords of Moorish Spain cannot be accidental given the close links between Constantinople and al-Andalus, but who influenced whom is a mystery. 3–6: early 11th century (Menologion of Basil II). 7: later 11th century (soapstone icon, Louvre). Blade forms include a pillow section (2, 4, 5, 7), and the fullered type with grooves ranging from narrow (1) to broad (3, 6). 3 and 4 have sleeves which encircle the mouth of the scabbard when sheathed. Pictures from the 11th century sometimes show what may be either a tassel or lanyard attached to the pommel or at the join between grip and pommel.

Once *hoplitai* or *skoutatoi* troops could march steadily, they would commence training with the pike, or *kontarion makron*, until they could efficiently execute all the manoeuvres known to the soldiery of Renaissance Europe. They had to be able to assemble the formation with an even front (command: *isason to metôpon*), to close on centre (command: *sfinxon*) or on the flank (command: *eis plagiou sfinxon*), to countermarch (command: *metallaxon*) and to change the formation's face by turning 180 degrees on the spot (command: *metaskêmatison*), as well as less exacting movements.

Whilst steadiness was the primary quality of the pike-armed *hoplitai*, the *peltastoi* and *menavliatoi* with their shorter spears underwent more athletic training to prepare them for their more mobile functions of skirmishing and of moving from a reserve position to reinforce weaknesses occurring in the formation. The side-arm combat skills of these men had to be at least equal to those of the *hoplitai*, if not more so, hence they must have used the same training exercises for these weapons.

The lights, or *psiloi*, practised using all manner of projectile, not merely the bow, but also hand darts (*martzobarbuloi*), javelins (*akontia/riptaria*) and the sling (*sfendobolon*). Leo goes so far as to recommend that they even practise throwing stones by hand. Archers were given the option of using the 'Roman draw', which had been with the thumb since late antiquity, or the 'Persian draw' with three fingers. Archery training involved not only practising to shoot full-sized arrows quickly and accurately at a spear shaft at long range, but also the more difficult technique of using the *sôlênarion*, whereby a small arrow, known as a 'fly' or 'mouse', was shot down a tube or channel to travel twice the distance of the larger missile. This weapon was used to lay down harassing fire on enemy formations, particularly cavalry, at long range, and so sureness of action and speed were more important than accuracy, though the *sôlênarion* could be a surprisingly accurate weapon when in practiced hands.

A siege scene with tents and traction trebuchet from the illuminated chronicle of Skylitzes. Although this manuscript was illustrated in Sicily in the 12th century, it drew heavily on East Roman sources of the previous centuries as well as contemporary observation. (Biblioteca Nacionale, Madrid)

Examples of warriors from ivory caskets showing realistic combat techniques. The position on the left might be described as 'first guard' given its evident derivation from the use of the old Roman *gladius*. The position on the right could be 'second guard' as the natural movement from the previous thrusting guard to a cutting position. (Illustration by David Irwin)

Two more warriors from 11th-century ivory carvings showing what might be characterized as 'third guard' and 'fourth guard'. The similarities between these and other depictions of this era and the later *Wapurgis Fechtbuch* (Royal Armouries MS I.33) may just be convergent evolution, but there are sufficiently intimate contacts between Germany and Constantinople in the 10th to 13th centuries to suggest that a direct transmission is just as likely. (Illustration by David Irwin)

In contrast to the ivories of individual warriors, which show open shield positions more characteristic of single combat, this carving of engagement on the front of an ivory casket shows both men in closed guards more typical of battlefield techniques. The man on the left is armed with a spear, while the swordsman has adopted a close covering to counter the speed and directness of the thrust or cast. (Illustration by David Irwin)

Maurikios and Leo recommend that this combination of drill and individual training should be supplemented by massed practice battles where sticks, or even whips, replaced striking weapons, and spears without points or substitutes of cane were used. Where the terrain allowed, clods of earth were to serve for projectiles in these clashes. Sometimes these practice battles were to take place on open ground, while at other times one unit would be sent to take and occupy a hilltop, holding it against another group sent against them. Leo places particular stress on this activity, suggesting that such battles should continue to be conducted even when the army was on campaign, if contact with the enemy was not imminent, and that the general himself should take a hand in acknowledging the efforts of

The author (right) demonstrating combat techniques reconstructed from middle Byzantine pictorial sources. (Author's Collection)

units who performed particularly well in these skirmishes, and in chiding those who did poorly.

Leo stresses the importance of training and constant practice in inuring the men to all manner of hardship, so we can be sure that in addition to specific combat training, the troops would have had to practise necessary adjunct skills such as making and striking camp, and particularly digging the ditches which continued to surround each expeditionary camp, just as they had done in the days of Caesar's legions.

An important part of training and of maintaining unit cohesion must have been the regular trooping of the colours. Each *meros* or *tourma* had a distinct square flag, which was then distinguished for each *droungos* and *vandon* by the addition of tails in various colours. It was essential that every man could instantly recognize the standard of his particular unit and division amongst the confusion of battle. Hence it seems likely that banners would also be used in the practice battles from time to time as well.

A training regimen as intensive and comprehensive as this, whenever it could be implemented and maintained, must have made units of the Roman Army who followed it fitter and more competent on a man-to-man basis than any of the peoples they had occasion to take the field against.

CONDITIONS OF SERVICE

During service

The conditions that governed the service of infantry troops in this period are far from clear from surviving sources. This is in part because they are never very specific about such details, and partly because they do not distinguish between infantry and cavalry in such matters. One possible conclusion from the latter is that there was no formal distinction between the two arms in their conditions of service.

As with all the Roman forces of this era, the infantry was divided into two broad categories – part-time and full-time. The part-time troops were probably sub-divided into two groups. One consisted of men who belonged to families that held military lands, or *strateia*, and therefore were obliged to keep in regular training, acquire and maintain some or all of their own equipment, and muster at the first call up. The other comprised men who had no formal military commitment, but like peasant levies in Europe would turn out for major expeditions or to resist incursions in their area.

The conditions of service for the levies would probably be restricted to their own province and immediately adjacent areas, and be strictly limited to short periods that would not compromise the productivity of their agricultural duties. Men of this category almost certainly served primarily as light troops using bows, slings and javelins, or perhaps as support staff – animal handlers, servants and so on – rather than as front line hand-to-hand combat soldiers. The reason for this is simply pragmatic. Less equipment was required for them or from them, and projectile skills are likely to have been maintained to some degree by normal hunting activities throughout the year. Where a higher level of

A

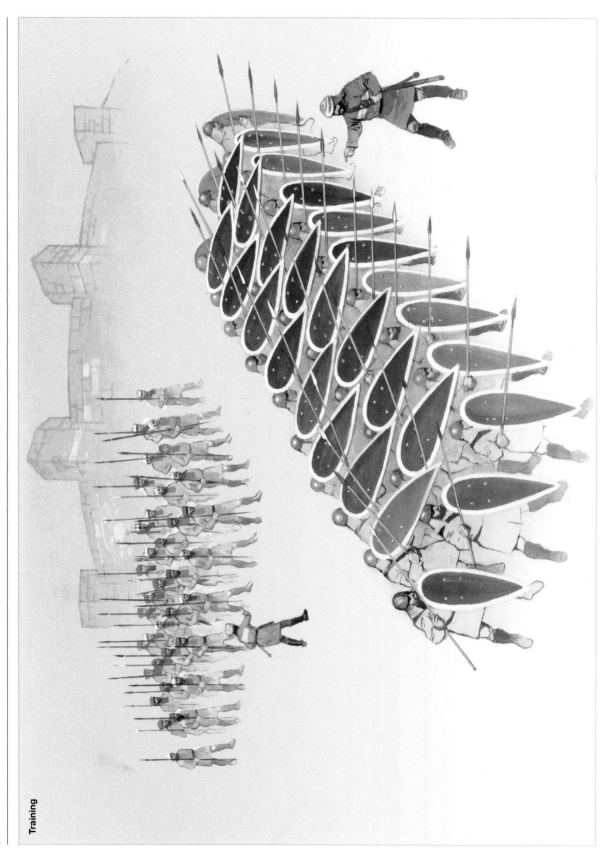

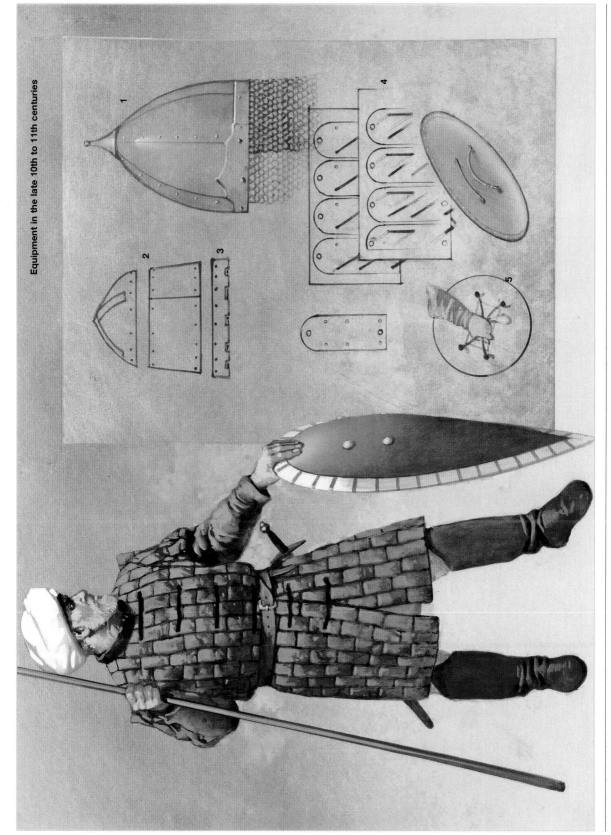

Battlefield formation in the late 10th century

D

Camp life on campaign in Armenia

E

Siege warfare

F

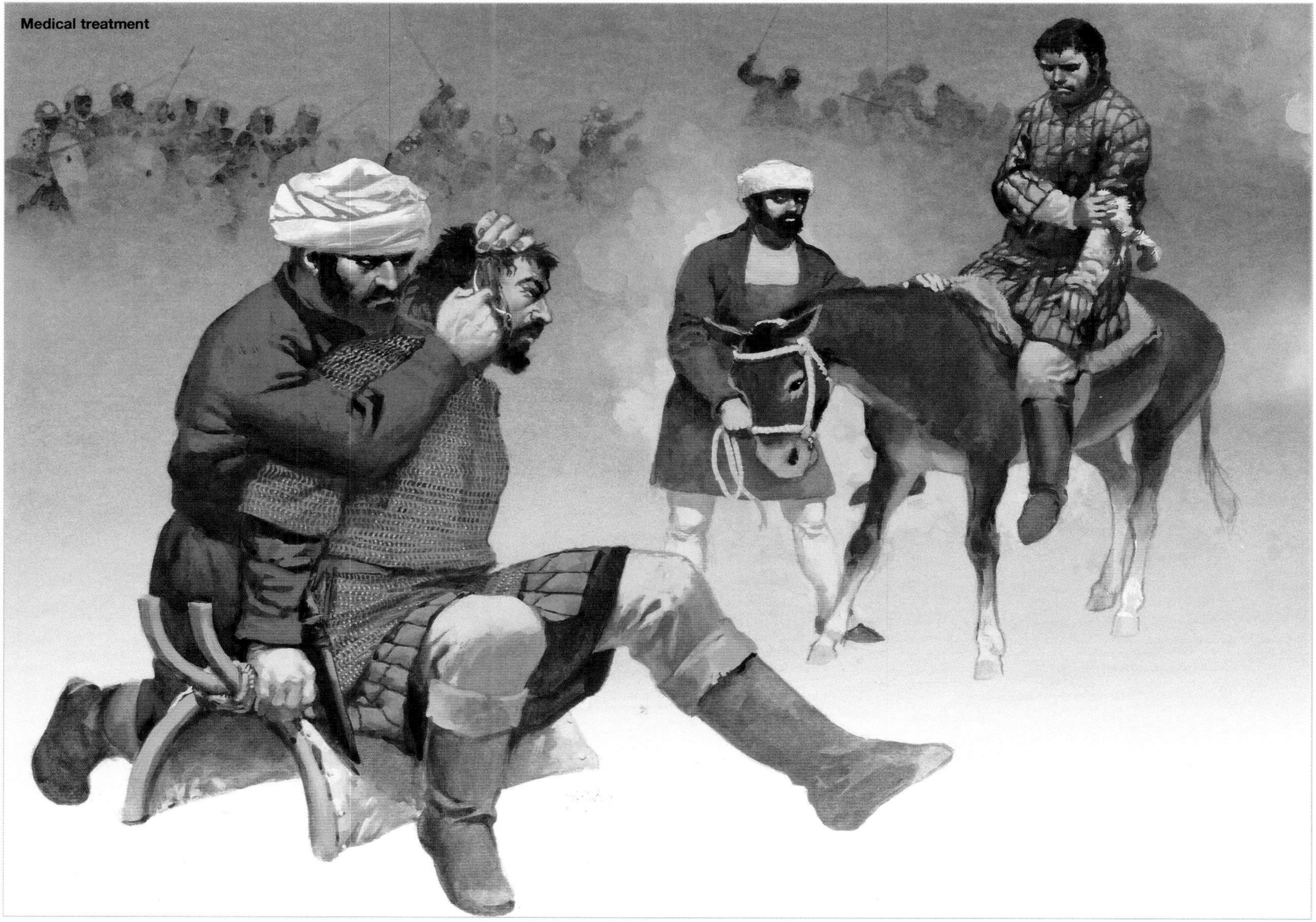

G

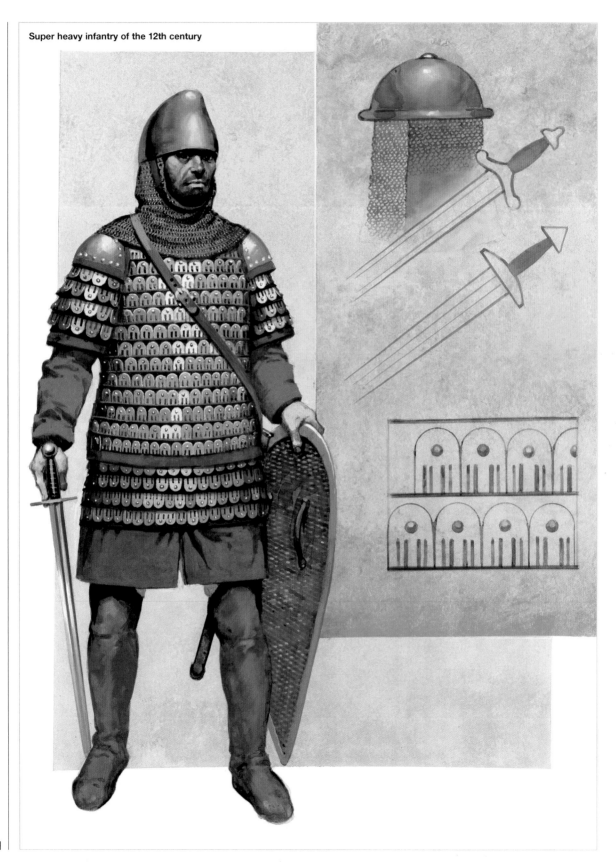

H

service was going to be demanded of them, the administrative unit calling them up would receive a special payment to acquire arms and armour for them.

Men discharging *strateia* obligations, or *strateioumenoi*, were expected to maintain themselves in training between campaigns. The local *stratêgos* had the responsibility of supervising the ongoing training of troops on the muster lists, so presumably from time to time he would assemble the enrolled troops to revise their drills. *Strateioumenoi* were also required to serve for longer periods and farther afield once a campaign was launched. At earlier stages, or when the expeditionary force was campaigning nearby, the estate bearing the *strateia* was expected to furnish some supplies for the man discharging the service; thereafter and farther afield the troops were sustained by forage and requisitioned supplies. Roman armies of this era did not normally campaign over winter, so the *strateioumenoi* enjoyed a standard demobilization of three months for the low season.

Troops recruited from a given locality were grouped together in common units. This was in part to ensure that they had things in common to bind them together through the privations of service, and partly to reduce the potential for infiltration by spies and saboteurs.

Full-time troops formed the defensive garrisons of major towns, and a larger force must have been stationed in the capital. As well as being on hand in preparation for sudden attacks, an important role for these garrison forces must have been to form a nucleus of well-trained and drilled troops to pass on a standard of performance to the *strateioumenoi* and levies once they were mobilized. As professional soldiers with no other means of support, they must have been maintained by the state, although if they served elsewhere they might well have brought equipment of their own, and in any case they would be sure to upgrade their gear whenever they were able, even if they had been initially equipped at state expense.

Unlike the early imperial era when a set period of service was expected, in this period the term of service seems to have been very pragmatic for both full-time soldiers and *strateioumenoi*. Men served as long as they were fit for duty, and sometimes even longer, for the manuals mention the need to review the muster rolls from time to time in order to weed out men who were no longer in a position to serve, as well as to add new recruits.

All troops received some payment for their service in addition to their maintenance. There seems to have been a common tendency for pay for long-term enrolled troops to be very irregular, as

A hero represented on a ceramic plate uses two swords to slay a beast. Such a combat technique would only have been a last resort on the battlefield, where the comprehensive protection of a shield was much more effective, but it shows the range of martial forms known at the time. (Illustration by David Irwin)

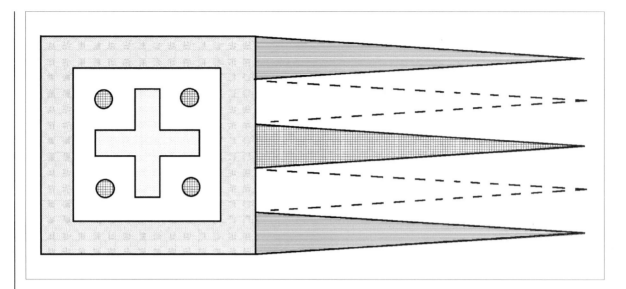

The standard form of the middle Byzantine military banner. The body represented the *meros* or *tourma* and carried some simple, often geometric emblem. The tails were colour coded for each sub-unit. The two outer tails probably represented the *droungos*, while the tails between (sometimes as many as five in especially large armies) bore a unique combination of colours for each banner.

indicated by outbreaks of unrest when pay was not forthcoming, and Constantine VII's attempt to set it on a four-year cycle. On special occasions, however, pay could be much more regular and frequent. The expedition to Crete in 949 paid 1 (gold) *nomisma* per month for four months to each ordinary soldier, apparently without distinction between cavalry and infantry.

Discipline was, of course, an essential element of military service, and all the manuals have substantial sections dealing with military laws and penalties. All the offences we would expect are noted: ignoring officers and orders; disobeying orders; desertion and betrayal to the enemy of plans or cities and fortresses. To these are added the theft, loss or unauthorized disposal of equipment and livestock, neglect of equipment, the theft of public money such as taxes and military levies and claiming allowances dishonestly.

For desertion and treachery the universal and time-honoured penalty of death was imposed. The basic penalty for many lesser infractions was scourging. This punishment was normally administered by the immediate superior officer of the offender. In certain cases a private's *dekarkhês* would also be punished for his fault, for instance if a man neglected his arms and armour whilst on leave. The actual quantity of lashes for any offence seems to have been left to custom, or the preferences of the officers concerned. Leo advises against excessive harshness as being likely to contribute to loss of morale and unrest in the ranks. Fines were also imposed for transgressions whose effects were financial. Thus, for example, a man who dishonestly claimed an allowance, such as for mobile service while the army was in winter quarters, was required to pay back twice the amount he had falsely gained.

On the positive side, a man who was honest and competent could look forward to earning promotion, sometimes to quite eminent rank, wherever he might have started. It should be noted, though, that good family connections did ease a man's path into the upper officer class, although this must have been a much more prevalent paradigm in the cavalry, simply by virtue of its being the more glamorous and expensive arm.

After service

The sources are largely silent about what became of surviving soldiers after they left the service, but some conclusions can be drawn from peripheral evidence. As noted above, the holders of *strateia* were liable to be called up from their farms for as long as they were physically capable of discharging the duty. Thereafter, they simply stayed at home while a younger or fitter member of the family took on the duty. The circumstances of demobilized tagmatic soldiers were much more diverse. The lack of any set period of service meant that a man might leave the army whilst still in his prime. Men were also, of course, invalided out of the service. Those who left half or not wholly disabled must have gone into any of the civilian occupations that they were capable of performing. In the early empire 45 years was the age at which a man became a *senex*, an old man, and marked the point at which he was discharged from the army if he had not yet completed the standard term. Since 40 was the maximum enlistment age recorded in the period of this study, it seems likely that 45 was still the retirement point. Another continuity is that tagmatic troops enjoying good health and having no other ties were settled on vacant military lands in the hope that they might establish families that would broaden the army's pool of manpower. Men who were discharged as invalid for whatever reason necessarily fell upon public or private charity. Religious institutions were the primary agencies for such charity, and monasteries must have been the refuge for many disabled or infirm elderly soldiers.

BELIEF AND BELONGING

The inhabitants of the Roman Empire as it endured in the East had a sense of identity that is hard for a modern Western person to understand. It was intimately bound up with religion, yet with an intensity that even medieval Westerners found hard to comprehend. For one thing, according to the Western Church's paradigm, issues of doctrine were to be thrashed out by silk-clad old men behind closed doors and then revealed to a grateful but acquiescent laity. In the Eastern Roman Empire, in contrast, the 'man-in-the-street' felt fully entitled to hold and express opinions on such matters, a situation of which the Eastern theologians themselves did not necessarily approve. In the 4th century the theologian Gregory (Grêgorios) of Nyssa remarked with disgust that a trip to the market or bathhouse could lead to a lecture on some obscure theological topic from such lowly fellows as the bread seller or bathhouse attendant. Indeed the outcome of some Church councils was as much determined by cudgels in back alleys as by elevated debate and negotiation in marble halls.

The compact made with the God of Christianity by Emperor Constantine at the battle of Milvian Bridge – 'In this sign you will conquer' – resonated throughout society, and right through the army. Yet the idea that with Constantine's bargain the Roman Empire became the vessel through which Christianity would be most perfectly expressed ultimately acted more to the army's detriment than to its advantage. On the one hand, there was the idea that if it were the Chosen Realm then God would defend it, provided its citizens were suitably pious, perhaps

even without the need for terrestrial armies. This was good for the cults of military saints and the Holy Virgin, but not necessarily good for army recruitment. The concept of 'proper piety' was also not entirely helpful. The habit of soldiers to assuage the stress of wartime service with drinking and fornication runs across cultural boundaries, and presented a constant problem within Orthodox religious parameters. Furthermore, Orthodox Christianity has never had anything like the concept of 'Holy War' that was contrived by the Church of Rome to justify crusading and the military-religious orders. One result of this was that homicide remained a sin, even when the victims were non-Christian enemies of Church and State. Hence, soldiers in the later Roman Army spent much of their campaigning time on penance, however token, for having committed murder. Such penance obviously could not be so exacting as to impair the men's functioning, so it must have been similar to the milder monastic practices of *xerofagia* and *hydroposia*, that is meals without meat and days without wine. Thus, being a soldier in the Eastern Roman Empire must sometimes have entailed being somewhat in an ideologically conflicted twilight zone, neither fully accepted by society, nor wholly supported by the Church. This feeling would be mitigated by the fact that the daily life of the army was punctuated by religious rites designed to ensure that the troops were aware of their important role in God's appointed empire, and would not die in a state of sin.

One of the most important foci for personal spirituality in Eastern Christianity has always been that of warrior saints, most notably Dêmêtrios, George and the two Theodores. Their cults must have had particular resonance for serving soldiers, despite the fact that most of them were martyred for refusing to fight (on behalf of pagan emperors). Warrior saints are the subject of the most commonly surviving type of less expensive icon, those carved of soapstone, where they are depicted with a degree of contemporary realism that is quite unlike other forms of Orthodox religious art. This suggests that their devotees felt a degree of affinity with them that was not shared with the more remote figures of Jesus or Mary. Warrior saints are also often found depicted on small, cast-bronze crucifixes that survive in some quantity. Such cheap talismanic jewellery must have been a common accessory across the army.

The picture is further complicated by the divergent lifestyles of the tagmatic and thematic armies. The part-time soldiering of the provincial forces must have left them with a direct sense of community – they could see that it was the homes of their families and neighbours they were defending. The nature of the *tagmata* would necessarily have broken that down as recruits left their communities across Rômania for the detached microcosm of barracks life in and around Constantinople and major cities. The sense of detachment from the urban civilian community can only have been enhanced by the fact that it fell to units of the army to suppress outbreaks of civil unrest in the capital and major cities. Such rioting was nowhere near as severe nor as brutally repressed in the middle Byzantine period as it had been earlier in the empire, yet still they were sometimes required to slaughter fellow citizens and fellow Christians who might even have been their neighbours or relatives.

So where did the Roman soldier of the 10th to 12th centuries find a sense of belonging? Sometimes undoubtedly it lay in shared loyalty to the emperor, at least when he had distinguished himself as a successful military commander, but many were ephemeral and did not do so. Ultimately, for the tagmatic armies especially, the sense of belonging must have fallen upon the institution of the army itself. The very organization of the army was designed to maximize this, with the continuing *kontouvernion* system forging bonds of familiarity as close as it is possible to be.

ON CAMPAIGN

The ancient Roman practice of organizing the infantry army by messes (Latin *contubernium*/Greek *kontouvernion*) had not lost its utility, and remained the core of campaign organization. Each mess comprised a file consisting of eight soldiers and a servant, who were quartered in one or two tents. The servant's primary duty was provisioning and cooking.

Tents of this era were of the pavilion type – round with a conical roof and walls and a single centre pole. One manual is very specific about the layout in such a tent. The file's provisions were stored in the centre. The men's bedding was then laid out around those, with their spears standing upright in the ground at the foot end of their beds, and their shield propped up against them with the handle facing the owner for ease and speed of access. The men's other items of kit, arms and armour and so on, were placed on the owner's left side. Presumably each man's personal kit included a *skoutellopinakon* – a set of bowl and cup, most probably in wood for durability and lightness. Pictures of this period show travellers' bedding as being quite like a thick sleeping bag, presumably with some sort of pad built into the bottom.

One wagon with its driver was assigned to each pair of files to carry the tents, the provisions and the additional equipment. This included tools, axes, mallets, mattocks, shovels, a sickle, cookware and a small hand-powered grain mill, as well as munition items like caltrops, arrows

Probably marking the transition
from the rectangular tents of
the earlier Roman Army to
round pavilion-style tents, the
6th-century manual *Concerning
Strategy* defines how the bedding
and equipment of a *kontouvernion*
should be laid out, as is shown
in this diagram. The soldiers'
equipment was laid out at the left
side of their bedding, while their
shields stood propped against
their spears at their feet. Their
rations and common equipment
were stored most safely at the
centre of the tent.

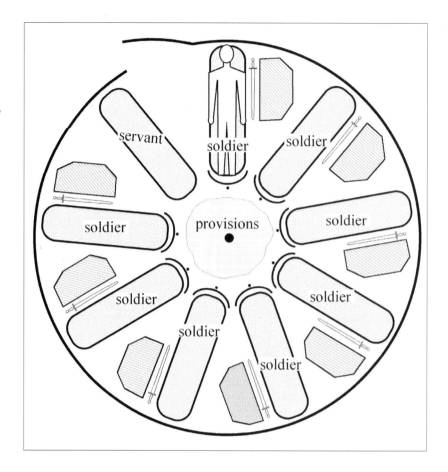

and spare bows. Where the terrain was too difficult, or supply was limited, pack animals were used in place of wagons.

Grains were the basis of campaign rations. They were initially carried both in prepared form and as flour. The mill in the stock of each double file was to process grains obtained by foraging as the expedition continued. The main preparation of grain was hardtack, called *paximata* or *paximadion*. This was coarse, double-baked bread. The simplest form was made from grain alone, but better types could include dried fruits and meats. More complex prepared rations are also described in the sources composed of a mixture of vegetables, nuts, seeds and honey. A marginal note in one 10th-century siegecraft manual describes one prepared ration in this way:

Another compound ration is made up thus. Take an Attic *hemiekton* of sesame, a *hemikhoun* of honey, a *kotul* of oil and a *khoinix* of peeled sweet almonds. Roast the sesame, grind and sift the almonds. Peel squill, cut away the roots and leaves and divide it up into small pieces. Put it into a bowl and pound it to a smooth paste. Next grind together an equal quantity of the squill paste and the honey and oil. Put into a pot and simmer it upon a charcoal fire. When it just starts to boil add the sesame and almonds and stir until it is entirely mixed. When it becomes firm, take it out of the pot and divide it into small pieces. Someone eating this, one piece in the morning and one in the afternoon,

Pilgrims lie on their bedrolls in the courtyard of a shrine. The motif of three unequal stripes is typical of such domestic textiles. Ordinary soldiers' bedding must have been very similar. Officers sometimes had the benefit of camp beds. (Monastery of Dionysiou, Mount Athos)

will have adequate nourishment. This food is good also for campaigning for it is sweet and filling and does not induce thirst.

A basic hot meal could be made from milled millet cooked up as a form of porridge. In richer seasons, troops might have the benefit of a common peasant staple still eaten today, *trakhanas*. *Trakhanas* is made of cracked wheat mixed with yoghurt, and was formed into balls or small loaves and left to dry in the sun. Like this it could keep for long periods

Although the manuals mention wagons, it is clear that very often the entire army's supplies were carried on mules, for much of the Balkans particularly had very poor roads. This is a detail of an 11th-century manuscript picture showing mules with their packsaddles. In camp, such saddles were commonly used as seats, the only furniture an ordinary soldier, or common traveller, had available. (Esphigmenou Monastery, Mount Athos)

and was boiled into a soup or stew to be eaten. Well-planned expeditions doubtless set off with supplies of preserved meat as well. Fresh supplies were purchased, requisitioned or foraged as the campaign progressed. Meal times were announced in camp by trumpet, although there are differing opinions in the sources as to how many meals there should be and when. In practice, set meals were probably a light breakfast and a dinner, with anything in between being an ad hoc affair arranged around whatever was the business of the time.

The practice of making marching forts is also continued in the manuals of this era. Surveyors were to go in advance of the army and lay out a camp in a suitable location. As with the old legions, such a camp was to be surrounded with a ditch and bank with L-shaped openings on each side. In addition, a strip of land was sown with caltrops in clusters of nine strung on a light chain and pegged down at one end for ease of recovery. In the 9th century General Nikêforos Fôkas (not the one who wrote the *Composition on Warfare*) invented a device akin to a tank-trap made of a tripod faced with a shield. One leg of this tripod was a spear with its point projecting outwards over the shield. These devices may have been used when a ditch and bank were not a viable option. Within these boundaries the tents of the various units were to be pitched together laid out in regular rows with streets in between. The substantial rope spread of the tents was to be fully interlaced, partly to keep the camp compact, but also as a security measure to restrict all traffic to the designated streets where it could be better overseen, and where focused defence could be organized in the event of incursion. The infantry, of course, bore the

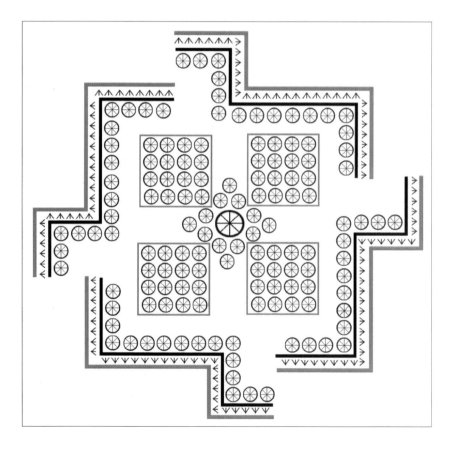

A schematic diagram of the layout of a marching camp according to an 11th-century manuscript, showing that the old Roman practices continued in use. The grey outer lines represent the ditch. The black inner lines represent the bank. The triangles are caltrops sown between them. The circles are tents. The central cluster is the residence of the commander and his staff.

brunt of the job of making camp, while the cavalry patrolled. This must surely have been the cause for widespread grumbling, but any real friction would have been moderated by the knowledge in contested territory that the wide-ranging screen of cavalry protected them from being caught unprepared armed only with shovels.

Once a camp was established and the day's activities were complete, the evening meal was followed by the singing of a hymn to the Trinity, the *Trisagion*, which initiated the night's curfew. During the night each file stationed a sentry outside its tent. This further ensured high levels of security, both in suppressing unauthorized movement around the camp, and in having almost 10 per cent of the infantry ready in arms in the event of a surprise attack. Passwords were required of anyone moving about the camp and were changed on a daily basis to prevent infiltration.

Expeditionary movements seem to have been episodic, with several days of marching with a daily encampment broken up by a day or days in one place for recuperation, repair or training exercises. There were also inevitably periods when the weather prevented planned movement. These intervals must have been quite miserable with the men mired under wet canvas, but would again be put to whatever good uses could be contrived. When camp was struck the cavalry would move off first so that their activities would not be obstructed by the less mobile infantry and baggage train.

The campaigning season was normally restricted to late spring to early autumn. Between those times the *strateia* troops would usually demobilize back to their farms, while the tagmatic soldiers retired to their home barracks. One notable exception to this rule happened in

For situations where it was not possible to set up a proper marching camp with bank and ditch, the 9th-century general Nikêforos Fôkas (ancestor of the manual-writing emperor) devised a form of palisade using the equipment the men normally carried, combined with what could reasonably be expected to be found locally. Three wooden spars were used to make an unequal tripod. The longer leg projected outward and was fitted with a spearhead. The tripod was then faced on its outer side with a shield. The gaps between these 'tank traps' would have been sown with caltrops as usual. (Author's Collection)

The harsh but magnificent landscape of Kappadokhia in winter. Leading to Armenia and Georgia to the north and Persian lands to the east, Kappadokhia was one of the main routes for armies on campaign. (Author's Collection)

the late 10th century when Nikêforos Fôkas decided to keep his expeditionary army in the field in Kappadokhia through the winter. The emperor had an entire subterranean barracks complex, comprising dormitories, refectories, storerooms and stables cut into the rock in accord with the ancient custom of the region. Such habitations are still commonly occupied to this day and these cosy shelters with their raised sleeping platforms and dining benches must have been a very welcome change from the draughts, damp, dirt and discomfort of long-term life under canvas.

EXPERIENCE OF BATTLE

The infantryman's experience of battle would have been a highly variable thing depending upon the circumstances. A field battle with infantry alone would not be the same as one with cavalry support. Likewise, the force mix of the enemy would change the character of the battle. A siege would, of course, be different again, whether in attack or defence. One thing would be consistent, however. The religious observances which were part of the army's daily routine were redoubled when battle was imminent. Thus, on the morning of a battle the prayer ritual was longer, and doubtless more heartfelt, with more of an emphasis on repentance for sin and making peace with God in the hope that a man might go into battle unconstrained by unfinished spiritual business. With such spiritual sustenance under the belt, the troops were

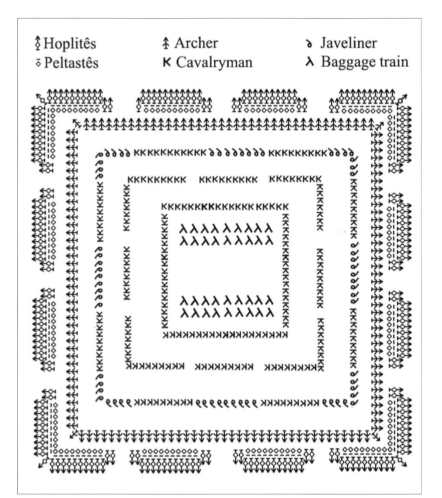

Key:
- ⚡ Hoplitês
- ○ Peltastês
- ⚔ Archer
- K Cavalryman
- ⟩ Javeliner
- λ Baggage train

A schematic diagram of the infantry square from an 11th-century manuscript.

provided with a solid meal before mustering to the field. Here the strength of the *kontouvernion* system must have been most valuable, as the men made their way to the front amidst the reassurance of the companions with whom they worked, ate, drank and slept.

In a field battle when the enemy did not have significant cavalry, or when the army could occupy the entire width of the battlefield with little danger of having its flanks turned, a linear formation was the norm. Each file or *kontouvernion* lined up one behind the other, with the *promakhos* or file leader at the front followed by his second and the *ouragos* or file-closer at the rear preceded by his second. These were normally the most heavily armoured men in the file, and between them stood more lightly armoured *skoutatoi* and projectile troops. The formation was not normally densely packed. Each man had 3 *podes* (approximately 90cm [1 yard]) in which to function. This could be closed up by one third if the unit had to form the *foulkon*, the old 'tortoise', against intense projectile barrage; however, such proximity would not be maintained longer than was absolutely necessary, as it would prevent the middle ranks from engaging once hand-to-hand combat commenced. Each *vandon* or two was also separated from its neighbours by a gap. The size of this gap would vary depending in the first instance upon whether the army had cavalry. If so, the gaps had to be large enough to allow the horsemen to charge out and retire, and would be protected by a designated cavalry unit called *defensôres*. If the infantry was operating alone, the gaps would be smaller, just big enough to pass light infantry skirmishers or the *menavliatoi* who protected the front from cavalry charges or the *daipotatoi* to recover the wounded.

Where the commander was confident of his flank and the terrain, he could take a more aggressive course, advancing the army to engage the foe. At the command '*Kinêson*' ('Move') the men would begin to march at their trained pace. It is notable that there is no command in the sources equivalent to 'At the double'. This because any attempt to move a large block of men at anything more than a steady walk inevitably causes it to break up, especially when they are using the longer pikes. Where the terrain was unsuitable the army would hold its ground and let the enemy come to it. This was a militarily safer option, but must have been psychologically risky at times, as the inaction could allow tension and apprehension to mount in the men which immediate action would forestall.

In situations where the flanks could not be secured and the opposing force had significant cavalry, the army was arrayed in a symmetrical square. The files formed up in the same manner, and again gaps were left for sallies and support, but the overall formation presented the same solid, well-protected face in all directions. This formation was necessarily less mobile than the line, but there would not often be reason to manoeuvre it since any cavalry present could necessarily outstrip its capacity to move.

Demonstration of how the first ranks of a formation would appear reinforced by a *menavliatos* and braced to repel cavalry according to Nikêforos Fôkas' *Composition on Warfare*. (Author's Collection)

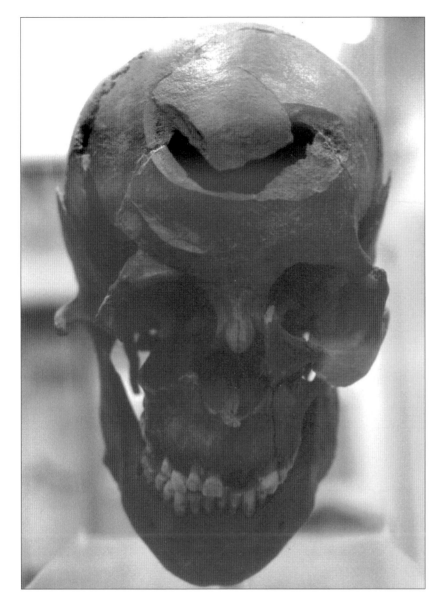

A grim testament to the effectiveness of ancient weaponry and the ferocity of battle. This man has suffered three cuts to the head: one over the right eyebrow, one across the bridge of the nose and one to the forehead. (Author's Collection)

In circumstances where both sides had significant cavalry, it is apparent that the primary burden of battle fell on them, and the role of the infantry formation was to be a human fortress, providing a secure base of operations from which the horsemen could launch their attacks. In such situations, the primary quality required of the troops was steadiness, and the experience of battle was in waiting and watching, interspersed by brief flurries of probably fairly inconclusive activity in fending off any of the enemy who had tried to pursue retreating Roman cavalry.

As the contending forces approached each other it was the archers who first came into play. They would commence with a barrage of long-range darts using the *sôlênarion* with the goal of deterring and disordering the oncoming units before they could begin to do any damage in return. As the enemy closed the range, the archers would begin to shoot full-size arrows, and after that slingers and javelineers

The walls of Ankyra were constructed around the year 900. Their pointed bastions are an unusual feature. Note the extensive use of recycled marble from earlier Roman buildings. (Author's Collection)

would come into play. When contact became imminent, the command 'Prothumos' ('Ready') instructed the troops to bring their weapons to the ready. In the main formation spears were the primary weapon. Even with the shorter spear (*kontarion*), four points project beyond the front of the line as it is first drawn up. When the attacking force was cavalry, the front of the formation would be reinforced by a rank of *menavliatoi* with their heavy spears (*menavlia*) braced with grounded butts. With the impetus of a cavalry charge broken, or the enemy infantry within range the foremost ranks applied their spears. Once the enemy began to break past the outermost points, the *promakhoi* would abandon their spears and fall back upon their hand weapons, swords and axes. Modern re-enactments show that this arrangement of a solid line of men armed with single-handed weapons and shields backed up by ranks of spearmen is highly effective, for those confronting them find it very difficult to defend against simultaneous striking and thrusting attacks in different openings.

No battle is one sided, however, and the Roman Army's unique strength is apparent in its arrangements for dealing with casualties. Approximately 100m (110 yards) behind the infantry battle line a field hospital was established. This was staffed by doctors and orderlies, and served by ambulance men (*daipotatoi* or *krivantai*). The *krivantai* probably had the use of mules from the baggage train for moving the wounded who could not walk. As the battle commenced, early casualties were caused by missiles. Slingers, while still mentioned in the sources, were much less used in this period, so piercing injuries from arrows were the norm. Once the lines were within striking distance the use of spears dominated the proceedings, producing stab wounds, with cutting injuries from swords and axes occurring less frequently. With most of the body covered by the tear-drop shield, the bulk of wounds would be predominantly in the head, face and throat, with fewer in such areas as the right shoulder and legs. Injuries to the head, face and throat tend to be more immediately incapacitating – psychologically, if not physically, although some, like scalp wounds which bleed copiously without necessarily being so acute, would allow men to return to the line quite quickly after basic treatment. It must have had a very steadying effect for the troops to see casualties being removed systematically from the combat area and from time to time returning after treatment to bolster the lines. It would be a dramatic contrast to virtually all of their enemies, amongst whom the wounded and dead merely lay where they fell and remained in the midst of the fighting.

After a victory the first item on the agenda was a ritual of thanksgiving to God and the burying of the dead. Some time afterwards came a review parade where those soldiers who had been seen to distinguish themselves in the battle were rewarded. It appears that some system of citation was in existence, as the manuals mention both 'honours and gifts'. Amongst the physical rewards mentioned are arms and armour and shares in the booty. The officers of well-performing units were likewise rewarded with promotion. At the same time, men who had failed to do their duty were punished. Extreme cowardice received the universal sanction, death, while flogging and fines were imposed for lesser failings.

It is often estimated that 15–20 per cent casualties was the breaking point for a medieval European army. This figure must have been higher for a Roman Army of this era, if only because the removal of the injured would somewhat disguise the issue, yet there were defeats. The ability of infantrymen to flee a battle is very limited, and they must have known that injury or death was as likely, if not more likely, during flight as it was in the battle line. Furthermore, the blinding atrocity against the Bulgars attributed to Basil II aside, it was not common practice to go to any great lengths to harry defeated enemies over great distances or to harm prisoners. Nor did medieval expeditionary armies have the capacity to maintain many prisoners. Hence, in the wake of a defeat, while men of status were pursued and taken into captivity, the lot of ordinary troops, whether they fled or were surrendered and released, was to straggle in the direction of home, or a base for regrouping, as best they could, bereft of equipment or supplies.

The experience of siege warfare was very different from this. The quality of Near Eastern fortification architecture and the precipitous and rocky sites normally chosen for medieval towns and castles meant that investment was the standard pattern for a siege. Then, for

The interior of the top gallery of one of the towers of the citadel of Ankyra (modern Ankara). The fighting area is very cramped, but, in a period prior to large-scale use of effective siege artillery by the empire's enemies, quite adequate. (Author's Collection)

defenders and attackers alike, it was a case of waiting to see whether one of the defenders might turn traitor, or which side would run out of supplies first, or whether a relieving force might appear. This waiting would be punctuated with bouts of conflict conducted with projectiles. The main exercise for a member of a besieging army might then just be stints of pulling on trebuchet ropes. In the absence of relief, the later part of the siege would entail increasing privation as food and water ran out. The defenders' only option at this point was surrender. An attacking force would begin to melt away, as the less resolute and loyal elements deserted, and eventually any sensible general would abandon the siege in order to preserve his army.

Where the site of the siege allowed more aggressive action, a familiar range of tactics were employed. Men less prone to claustrophobia would be set to undermining the fortification, and a variety of drills and rams could be deployed against areas of wall that looked weak. Lower and more accessible portions of the wall would be the subject to storming attempts. In addition to wheeled towers with draw-bridges, the 10th-century siegecraft manuals show some very sophisticated lifting platforms to deliver troops to wall tops. Such siegeworks added the danger of injury or death from cave-ins, wall collapses and falls to all normal battlefield risks.

MUSEUMS AND RE-ENACTMENT

Most of the core territory of the Eastern Roman Empire in this era is now contained within the boundaries of the modern state of Turkey. Modern Turks are ambivalent, to say the least, about this portion of the Roman Empire, seeing it as 'tainted' with Hellenism, and as a result archaeology of non-Turkish material in Anatolia is neglected and scanty. In any case, the export of all archaeological antiquities is prohibited. Greece and the Balkans do yield a certain amount of material, but little of substance reaches the open market. Hence, while small and non-specific items such as buckles are often available to collectors, nothing of military significance (except, perhaps, the occasional arrowhead) is to be found on the antiquities market.

Similarly, material in museum collections is also very sparse. The maritime museum at Bodrum in Turkey holds the significant assemblage from the 11th-century Serçe Limani shipwreck, which includes some weapons and tools. Other weaponry is very rare. There are just two helms of the period surviving. The 10th-century 'Yasenovo helm' is held in the archaeological museum at Kazanlik, Bulgaria, while a 13th-century parade kettle-hat inlaid with busts of saints is kept in the Hermitage Museum, St Petersburg. Weapons and pieces of lamellar found in the ruins of the Great Palace by a British excavation in the 1930s are held in the Byzantine Museum in Istanbul, but may not presently be on display.

In contrast, the physical bulwarks of the empire necessarily survive extensively. The walls of Constantinople have been subject to extensive restoration over the last 15 years (although this has sometimes distorted the form of certain elements) and are extensively accessible over most of their length. There is a substantial and interesting later fortress at the

A large garrison fortress guarding the north end of the Bosforos, probably built in the Komnenian era. Its larger size and strength are a response to the greater threats of the 12th century, both from larger armies and better artillery, and from the greater economic strength of the empire in this period. (Author's Collection)

north end of the Bosforos readily visited by regular ferries, while Nikaia (modern Iznik) and Thessaloniki retain extensive remains of their city walls. The citadel of Ankyra (modern Ankara), built in the 9th century, is a fascinating study of the extensive re-use of antique marble, and has a distinctive form. Kappadokhia has a number of fortresses, and a subterranean barracks complex built in the 10th century. Kilikia has a wide array of quite well-preserved buildings of this era with military character ranging from strong houses to major fortresses, although generally their present form derives from Armenian work.

As this is a relatively obscure and traditionally somewhat denigrated era of history, there are, as yet, few avenues for re-enactment or recreation of the Roman Empire of this period. Larger, broad-spectrum groups such as 'the Vikings' (UK and USA) and the 'Society for Creative Anachronism' (USA and international) embrace it as a minority interest. The 'New Varangian Guard' (Australia and elsewhere) is one well-established group with a Byzantine focus, although, as its name indicates, it leans more to the mercenary forces that converged upon Constantinople than to native Romans. The 'Hetaireia Palatiou', or 'Palace Company', is a group in Britain that recreates aspects of the court milieu such as ceremonial and military guard activities, while 'La Tagma de Byzance' in France focuses on the late Byzantine era.

GLOSSARY

The transliteration of Greek in modern times has been traditionally contaminated by influences imported from post-Classical Latin. In this volume, the transliteration has been based upon the pronunciation of Greek as it was spoken in the period covered, which was already largely similar to modern usage. Hence, beta = v, and eta (ê) and omega (ô) are pronounced as i and o respectively. Kh is a fricative or heavily accented aspirant like the ch in the Scottish 'loch'. Forms given are usually singular. The forms of Greek plurals are variable depending upon gender, but are thus: masculine ~os>~oi, ~ês>~ai, ~ôr>~ores, ~ôn>~ones – feminine ~a>~ai – neuter ~on>~a, ~a>~ata.

alakation trebuchet. Traction-powered trebuchets were introduced from China in the 6th century, while the counterweight trebuchet was invented in the Eastern Roman Empire in the 12th century.

daipotatos (Latin *deputatus*) field medic who recovered the wounded and returned them to treatment centres. Also *despotatos*, *dipotatês* and **krivantês**

dekarkhion the basic unit of the infantry army. Eight men comprising seven combat troops, including a **dekarkhos**, and a servant, who served, messed and slept together. See also file/**kontouvernion**

dekarkhos commander of a **dekarkhion**. Previously *lokhagos*

droungarios commander of a **droungos**

droungos a unit of between 1,000 and 3,000 men, commanded by a **droungarios**. Also **taxiarkhion** and *khiliarkhion*

file a group of troops who stood one behind another in battle to make up the depth of the formation. Previously a group of 16 men called a **lokhos**, but by the middle Byzantine era a **dekarkhion**

foulkon an infantry formation involving full coverage with interlocked shields – the old Latin *testudo* or tortoise

hekatontarkhês commander of 100 men. Also **kentarkhês** and **kentêriôn**

hetaireia Greek for 'company'. Units of the metropolitan tagma. Previously *skhola*

hoplitês the most heavily armoured front-line infantryman. Also *kontaratos* (spearman) or *skoutatos* (shieldbearer)

hypodêmata general term for footwear used for the thigh boots of 10th-century infantry

iatros doctor

kampotouva padded leggings

kavadion padded arming coat worn by infantry in lieu of solid armour. This term was also applied to civilian coats. See **zava**

kentarkhês commander of 100 men. Also **kentêriôn** and **hekatontarkhês**

kentarkhion a unit of 100 (Latin *centurium*)

kentêriôn (Latin *centurion*) Commander of 100 men. Also **kentarkhês** and **hekatontarkhês**

klivanion 1: a corselet of **lamellar**; 2: lamellar as a fabric of armour

komês 'count'. Commander of a **vandon** (banner)

kontarion spear. ~ *mikron*: a shorter spear that was lighter than a **menavlion**. ~ *makron*: a pike

kontouvernion the old Latin *contubernium* – a **dekarkhion** which served, messed and slept together as a somewhat self-contained unit

krivantês field medic who recovered the wounded and returned them to treatment centres. Also **daipotatos**, *despotatos* and *dipotatis*

lamellar armour made of plates of metal, horn or leather fastened together with cordage, or, in the Eastern Roman Empire uniquely, a mixture of rivets and cordage, in which the rows of plates overlap upwards

lokhagos 'file leader'. Traditionally commander of eight fighting men forming a **file** or **lokhos** making up the depth of the battle formation. Effectively superseded in this period by the term **dekarkhos**

lokhos see **file** and **dekarkhion**

lôrikion usually a mail shirt. ~ *alusidôton*: literally 'chain armour'. ~ *folidôton*: a shirt of scales

mandatôr functionary who carried orders from the High Command to front line officers

manganarios an artilleryman. See **vallistarios**

menavlion shorter, heavyweight spear used to break cavalry charges and for skirmishing

minsouratôr	surveyor sent ahead of the army on campaign to lay out the campsite. Also *minsôr*
paramêrion	single-edged slightly curved sword hung horizontally from either a belt or shoulder strap and used by all types of troops
paximata	also *paximadion*. Hardtack made of course-ground whole flour double baked, and possibly also containing other dried foods such as fruit and meat
pektorarion	coloured cloth band tied around the chest to signal rank
peltastês	second-rank infantryman who might be as well armoured as a **hoplitês**, but usually carried a smaller shield and the shorter **kontarion**. Sometimes synonymous with **hoplitês**
psilos	light infantryman, commonly an archer, sometimes a slinger or javelineer. He carried a small buckler, wore no armour and might only have a single-edged short sword as a secondary weapon
skoutarion	general term for shield
sôlênarion	wooden tube or channel used to shoot small arrows to harass the enemy at a great distance
spathion	(Latin *spatha*) a double-edged straight sword used by all types of troops. The standard form was hung vertically from a shoulder strap like the ancient *gladius*. Another type used for lighter armoured troops and for parade purposes was hung horizontally from a belt: ~ *zôstikion*
stratêgos	'general'. Commonly a *stratêgos* served as a provincial governor (see **thêma**), but he might serve in a purely military capacity
strateia	The arrangement whereby a family held and farmed land owned by the state in exchange for military service by a designated male.
tagma	principal unit of the standing army, or the army in general
taxiarkhês	commander of a *taxiarkhia*
taxiarkhion	see **droungos**
thêma	province. By the middle Byzantine period thematic organization was somewhat tenuous, but a thematic **stratêgos** or *doux* was expected to raise troops for a campaign in his region
therapeutês	(male) nurse or orderly in a field hospital or dressing station
thureos	large infantry shield – pavise
tourma	unit of 3,000–9,000 men. Commanded by a **tourmarkhês**
tourmarkhês	commander of a **tourma**
tzikourion	battle axe, commonly with one standard blade and a hammer, spike or knife-like blade
vallistarios	(Latin *ballistarius*) an artilleryman manning a **vallistra**
vallistra	(Latin *ballista*) Arrow-firing torsion *vallistrai* were carried on campaign, while stone-throwing machines were used from fortifications
vandon	'banner'. A unit of 200–400 infantry divided into *kentarkhia*
voukinatôr	(Latin *bucinator*) trumpeter
zava	in earlier usage flexible body armour which might be a padded arming coat worn in lieu of solid armour, or a shirt of mail or scales. By the 10th century it had been supplanted by consistent use of more specific terms – **kavadion**, **lôrikion** etc – and had come to mean mail pieces used to supplement more solid armour, usually for cavalry

BIBLIOGRAPHY

Primary sources in translation

Constantine Porphyrogennêtos, *Three Treatises on Imperial Military Expeditions*, John F. Haldon (ed. and tr.), Verlag der Österreichischen Akademie der Wissenschaften, Vienna (1990)

Maurice, *Maurice's Strategikon*, George T. Dennis (tr.), University of Pennsylvania Press, Philadelphia (1984)

Maurikios, *Das Strategikon des Maurikios*, George T. Dennis (ed.) and Ernst Gamillscheg (tr.), Verlag der Österreichischen Akademie der Wissenschaften, Vienna (1981)

Nikêforos Fôkas, *Composition on Warfare* (commonly called *Praecepta Militaria*), Eric McGeer (ed. and tr.), *Sowing the Dragon's Teeth*, Dumbarton Oaks, Washington (1995)

Three Byzantine Military Treatises, George T. Dennis (tr.), Dumbarton Oaks, Washington (1985)

Vegetius, *Epitoma de Rei Militaris*, Leo F. Stelton (ed. and tr.), Peter Lang, New York (1990)

Untranslated primary sources

Anonymous, *De Obsidione Toleranda*, Hilda Van Den Berg (ed.), E. J. Brill, Leiden (1947)

'Leonis Imperatoris Tactica', *Patrologia Graeca*, 107, cols 672–1120, Budapest (1917–1922)

Sylloge Tacticorum, Alphonse Dain (ed.), Société d'édition 'Les Belles lettres', Paris (1938)

General works

Birkenmeier, John W., *The Development of the Komnenian Army, 1081–1180*, Brill, Leiden (2002)

Cheveddin, Paul F., 'The Invention of the Counterweight Trebuchet: A Study in Cultural Diffusion', *Dumbarton Oaks Papers*, 54 (2000)

Dawson, Timothy, '*Kremasmata, Kabbadion, Klibanion*: Some Aspects of Middle Byzantine Military Equipment Reconsidered', *Byzantine and Modern Greek Studies*, 22 (1998), pp.38–50

———, '*Suntagma Hoplôn*: the Equipment of Regular Byzantine Troops, *c.*950 to *c.*1204', David Nicolle (ed.), *Companion to Medieval Arms and Armour*, Boydell and Brewer, London (2002), pp.81–96

———, '*Klivanion* Revisited: An Evolutionary Typology and Catalogue of Middle Byzantine Lamellar', *Journal of Roman Military Equipment Studies*, 12/13 (2001/2)

———, 'Fit for the Task: The Dimensions of Byzantine Military Equipment in Manuals of the Sixth to Tenth Centuries', *Byzantine and Modern Greek Studies* (forthcoming)

Haldon, John F., 'Some Aspects of Byzantine Military Technology from the Sixth to the Tenth Centuries', *Byzantine and Modern Greek Studies*, I (1975), pp.11–47

———, *Recruitment and Conscription in the Byzantine Army c.550–950*, Österreichischen Akademie der Wissenchaften, Vienna (1979)

———, *Byzantium at War*, Osprey, Oxford (2002)

Kolias, Taxiarchis, *Byzantinische Waffen*, Österreichischen Akademie der Wissenchaften, Vienna (1988)

———, 'Essgewohnheiten und Verplegung im Byzantinischen Heer', *Byzantinos: Festschrift fur Herbert Hunger zum 70. Geburtstag*, eds., W. Hörander *et al.*, Vienna, pp.193–202

Treadgold, Warren, *Byzantium and its Army: 284–1081*, Oxford University Press, Oxford (1995)

COLOUR PLATE COMMENTARY

A: AT THE BEGINNING OF THE 10TH CENTURY

Leo and the anonymous author of the *Syllogê Taktikôn* anticipated a high level of equipment for the infantry. In fact the heaviest foot soldier, the *hoplitês*, was ideally to have almost identical armour to a heavy cavalryman. His plumed helm may well have been intended to have a covering for the face like that of a cavalryman. His body armour was to be a shirt of mail, or of scales made of metal or horn, or a corselet of lamellar similarly made of metal or horn. The form of lower limb protection in use at this time is not clear. It may still have been solid metal, as is suggested by some pictorial sources, but a splinted construction as is seen elsewhere at the time is also likely. Where resources did not stretch to such high-quality defences, the minimum alternative was a heavily padded coat with sleeves slit at the elbow and turned back to the shoulder for freedom of movement (1). Oval shields were still in use, but had been largely superseded by the tear-drop shape. The better pictures show that these were curved in two dimensions, and were probably made on a base of basketwork and covered with hide – a very durable construction. Concave round shields were also common. The grips of these shields were two lengths of rope or leather fastened through loops fixed into the body of the shield (See plate C). Each of these soldiers carried a spear, either the great *kontarion* of 4m (nearly 4½ yards) or more, the 'small' *kontarion* of about 2.5m (4¾ yards) or the *menavlion*, a heavy 2.5m (4¾ yard) weapon used for breaking cavalry charges and skirmishing. Side arms consisted of a slightly curved, single-edged sword called a *paramêrion* or the straight double-edged *spathion*. Either of these could be hung from a waist belt or shoulder strap, with a shoulder strap being used over more rigid armours like scale and lamellar, while the belt suspension was employed over flexible forms of protection like padded coats or mail shirts. A *tzikourion*, an axe with two identical or different blades, was carried holstered on the right hip (2). The second ranking infantry, the *peltastês*, had only slightly inferior armour to the *hoplitês*, and the same level of armament where possible.

B: TRAINING

It is hard to assess from the sources and evidence just how well or frequently trained the infantry of this period generally were. The standing tagmatic units were probably as well practised as any Roman troops had ever been. Individual training must still have been founded on 'square bashing', as well as exercises at the post with practice hand weapons. Marching drill was more essential than ever since handling the long pike that had been reintroduced in the 9th century in the formations and manoeuvres described in the manuals could not be done without complete mastery of this regular motion. The manuals also record the continuity of time-honoured Roman tactics such as the tortoise, now called the *foulkon*. The training of provincial levies was doubtless much less systematic, perhaps frequently relying on a crash course of intensive drilling in the interval between

their being called up for a campaign and being committed to battle. The *Taktika* of Leo speaks of training drills and practice battles taking place during static periods while an army was on the march, possibly to compensate for the low levels of training which might prevail in a newly mustered army.

C: EQUIPMENT IN THE LATE 10TH TO 11TH CENTURIES

When the successful general and emperor Nikêforos Fôkas wrote his manual in the third quarter of the 10th century his expectations for the basic equipment of the infantry were much more modest than those of Emperor Leo. Fôkas did not expect the troops to have anything more than the padded coats which were for Leo merely an expedient to fall back upon. Fôkas says these coats are to be made of 'coarse silk padded with cotton wadding as thick as can be stitched', and, like Leo, describes the sleeves very precisely, but differently, invoking a form which goes back to the earliest types of Persian coat in which the opening is in the armpit rather than the elbow (see the photograph on page 8). Nor did he expect them necessarily to have metal helms, but thick turbans wrapped over heavy felt caps. This is not so surprising when one sees that he envisaged them fighting in dense blocks with long pikes and so perhaps never coming within arm's length of the enemy. Skirmishing troops like the *menavliatoi* undoubtedly did aim to have better protection including helmets. The so-called 'Caucasian' style of helm (1) was also descended from ancient Persian precursors, but becomes much more prevalent throughout the region in the late 10th century. The 'Yasenovo helm' (2) is a unique survival, but it can be seen from various pictorial sources that the type was quite widely in use through the 11th century and probably beyond. Its cross-banding is offset towards centre front and back to cover the points most commonly struck – an expedient first seen in Roman helms during the Dacian campaign of the early 2nd century. The mail hanging of the Yasenovo helm and many of the surviving Caucasian helms involves threading the mail onto a wire which runs through a channel formed inside the rim of the helmet (3). If they should have been lucky enough to have lamellar body armour they would have benefited from a further stage in the technological evolution that was unique to Vyzantion, whereby the form of construction in which plate was laced to plate was replaced by fixing the plates to a leather band either by laces or, as here, by rivets (4). Art works surprisingly often show the insides of shields and indicate that the grip method stayed quite constant throughout the period, with two cords or leather straps fixed through loops set in the body of the shield (5).

D: BATTLEFIELD FORMATION IN THE LATE 10TH CENTURY

The infantry formation advocated by the highly experienced general and later emperor Nikêforos Fôkas for open field battles where cavalry was a significant threat is uncannily prescient of tactics used in the 17th century in Western

Metal finds from the 1204 destruction layer of the Great Palace in Constantinople included a spearhead, arrowheads and lamellar plates. (After *The Great Palace of the Byzantine Emperors*, eds Brent, Macaulay and Stevenson, 1947, pl. 58)

Europe. Whether this is merely a case of the most effective solution to the danger from heavy cavalry being independently reinvented, or whether Fôkas' manual made it to the West, as that of Vegetius is known to have done, is not clear. Fôkas proposed drawing up the infantry army as a hollow square with each face one file of seven men deep, with archers behind the *hoplitai* and the *menavliatoi* held in reserve in the centre. The faces of the square had gaps to allow sallies by the *menavliatoi* or light troops. Where the army was big enough, those gaps would also admit cavalry which could regroup and rearm inside the formation. Where an army had the advantage of a battlefield with secure flanks, a linear formation would be used, but would still be drawn up in essentially the same way as a single face of the square – a file deep with gaps and the skirmishers, lights and cavalry in reserve behind. Whether line or square, the files were arranged with three *hoplitai* or *peltastai* in front carrying long *kontaria*, then two or three archers, then again one or two *hoplitai* or *peltastai* at the rear waiting to fill gaps caused by casualties.

E: CAMP LIFE ON CAMPAIGN IN ARMENIA

The concern for the careful organization of marching camps that is well known from the early Roman imperial era continues with the manual writers of the 10th century. The camp was still to be laid out as a square with defined roads in a grid pattern within a bank and ditch whenever possible. In addition to that, or in place of it when it proved impractical, the camp was surrounded by a 'minefield' of caltrops and tripods with spearheads projecting outwards. The broad rope spread of the pavilions in use by this time meant that in order to retain the size of the camp within

more manageable proportions, and to force traffic onto the designated routes where it could be kept under surveillance, the ropes of the tents were interlaced. Each pavilion housed a file, while smaller triangular tents housed officers and other functionaries. Each file was to have a sentry posted outside its tent, when not committed to battle. Two files shared logistic support – a wagon with their baggage when on the move, and catering arrangements in camp. In this scene most of the troops are away on a training exercise. Besides the sentries and servants, there is a scattering of men left behind who have been excused from active duties, usually due to illness or injury. The manuals stress that down time in camp was to be used for keeping equipment clean, polished and in good repair. The sources suggest that it was not uncommon for officers to carry furniture such as beds and chairs with them, much to the theorists' disapproval, but the ordinary troops had to make do with whatever they could improvise. Pack saddles were very commonly used as seats during this period, just as in more recent times. The pervasiveness of Orthodox Christianity notwithstanding, Roman soldiery of this period were no less in need of physical indulgences and impious distractions as those of any era, so, again much to the theorists' disapproval, expeditionary forces drew camp followers and personal services from the local residents of the regions through which they passed. The clothing of this woman hawking wine around the camp indicates that she is from the native Armenian population rather than from some other ethnic group following the army.

F: SIEGE WARFARE

Siege warfare is most often thought of from the point of view of the attackers, but the defence of cities and settlements must have been one of the more frequent duties of any infantry force. There was an art to effective defence as well as to attack, which earned its own manual written in the 10th century. Even just waiting out the investing army required careful preparation to ensure sufficient supplies of provisions and materiel were laid on for the remaining defenders and populace. Active countermeasures could both blunt the attackers' ability to prosecute the siege and hasten the day when they decided the venture was costing more than it was worth. Some siege machinery had originally been developed for defence more than attack, such as the various forms of arrow-shooting *vallistrai* which had originated amongst the ancient Greeks. The Roman Army's capacity for building and operating torsion artillery had by no means been lost with the fall of the Western part of the empire. Mikhail Psellos tells us that one *vallistra* crew defending a city in the early 11th century was sufficiently skilled and accurate that it could put the fear of mortal danger into a lone cavalryman mocking the defenders from the outside the walls and force him to withdraw. Both arrow- and stone-casting machines were still in use. Greek Fire is best known as a naval weapon, yet from time to time it was used defensively on land in situations where the collateral damage would be minimal. The precise form of Greek Fire siphons is a matter of guesswork, since the original descriptions and depictions are far from precise. This one is based upon the theory of Haldon and Byrne. The traction catapult had come into Roman use in the 6th century, but its inherent inaccuracy and severely limited throw-weight meant that it was never very effective as an offensive weapon. Here one is being put to defensive use, not only throwing solid projectiles, but also simultaneously ridding the city of its waste and spreading discomfort and disease amongst the besiegers by casting containers of excrement into the enemy camp. Every soldier was expected to be competent with a bow, and in defending a town this skill would, for the *skoutatoi*, mostly take precedence over their hand-to-hand combat skills.

G: MEDICAL TREATMENT

Another of the major areas in which the Roman Army was far ahead of its contemporaries was in the matter of medical treatment. With a heritage of medical lore running continuously back to classical Greece, the doctors who travelled with the army were as good as any in the world, and probably more so in terms of the particular needs that prevailed in the military lifestyle. In time of battle the access

to these skills was as well organized as anything else. A specific body of men, called *despotatoi* or *krivantai*, had the function of recovering wounded men from the battlefield and returning them to field hospitals behind the lines for treatment. There they were attended to by both physicians (*iatroi*) and orderlies or male nurses (*therapeutai*). The sources tell us that the *despotatoi* had their own mounts to carry the wounded, and that all medical staff were unarmed. Doctors of the Graeco-Roman world were adept at suturing lacerations and setting limb fractures, while amputation remained the only viable course where limbs had suffered severe tendon, ligament or joint damage. There was also a detailed body of lore for dealing with abdominal wounds, although this was acknowledged to be much less effective than treatments for other injuries. It is very likely that any solid armour that wounded troops were wearing would be stripped off immediately behind the battle lines, both for ease of transport and treatment and so that it might be taken up by any under-armoured troops still in the fight.

H: SUPER HEAVY INFANTRY OF THE 12TH CENTURY

The 10th century had achieved a pinnacle of sophistication in arms and armour that did not leave much room for improvement in the context of pre-gunpowder combat. The 11th and 12th centuries did see some changes, but they were due mainly to the benefits of economic growth rather than to significant technological change. At the bottom end, sources tell us that a heavy turban and padded coat were the lowest form of protection a foot soldier employed. At the top end, it seems that greater resources allowed lamellar armour to be more available to the infantry than it had been previously. There had also been changes in both the construction and use of lamellar. The single-riveted, two-lace construction was still in use, but it had undergone several modifications. The use of two rivets per plate had been tried in the early 11th century, but by the 12th century had been supplanted by four suspension laces. The splinted upper sleeves of the 10th century had been replaced by sleeves of inverted lamellar, or occasionally scales. One major innovation can be seen here which makes this armour specific to infantry, namely the inverted lamellar skirt running continuously across the lower belly and groin, thus covering one of the most vulnerable areas left by the traditional *klivanion* construction, which catered mainly for cavalry. The Phrygian cap-style helmet, known since antiquity, had a period of renewed popularity in the 12th century, which transcended ethnic boundaries. The precise shape of Phrygian cap helms is hard to tell from the manuscript pictures of this time. The sharply creased ridge across the front of this type makes a very rigid and impervious shape. In this period we begin to see thigh-length boots being depicted, although of the same type as shown in Turkish sources, with a flap pulled up over the knee and fastened up to the trouser cord.

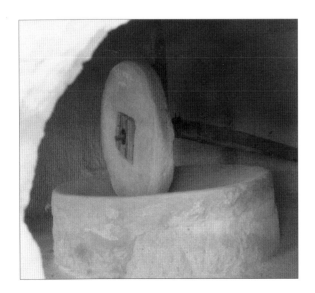

A mill built in a man-made cave cut from the soft rock of Kappadokhia. Whole cities were carved out this way in the middle ages, and in the middle of the 10th-century Emperor Nikêforos Fôkas had a complete barracks complex cut this way for one expedition that was to spend the winter on campaign in the region. (Author's Collection)

INDEX